THE
CHURCHES'
WAR ON POVERTY

THE
CHURCHES'
WAR ON POVERTY

LYLE E. SCHALLER

ABINGDON PRESS
NASHVILLE   NEW YORK

THE CHURCHES' WAR ON POVERTY

Copyright © 1967 by Abingdon Press

All rights in this book are reserved.

No part of the book may be reproduced in any manner
whatsoever without written permission of the publishers ex-
cept brief quotations embodied in critical articles or reviews.
For information address Abingdon Press, Nashville, Tennessee.

Library of Congress Catalog Card Number: 67-11014

SET UP, PRINTED, AND BOUND BY THE
PARTHENON   PRESS,   AT   NASHVILLE,
TENNESSEE, UNITED STATES OF AMERICA

To
Erling Peterson
W. B. Waltmire
Kenneth E. Whitney

PREFACE

During the first fifteen years following the end of
World War II the primary focus of the main-line Protestant
churches in America was on the suburban middle-class family.
This was reflected in the emphasis on new church development by denominational home mission boards. It was reflected
in the migration of hundreds of central city churches to the
suburbs as the members of the congregation first moved
their own places of residence and later voted to take their
churches with them to the security of suburbia. It was
reflected in the criticisms of Gibson Winter and others who
described the "suburban captivity of the churches."

At the same time that the major efforts of American
Protestantism were being directed toward the people in
suburbia, hundreds of other churches and church-sponsored
agencies were continuing the centuries-old Christian ministry
to the poor, the deprived, the dispossessed, and the destitute.
This ministry was being conducted in an almost total absence
of publicity and frequently with limited funds, but usually

with unlimited dedication. It is difficult to overstate the importance of this work during those years when three fourths of the American people were living in prosperity and poverty was a forgotten issue. These efforts by the churches against poverty and on behalf of the poor must not be forgotten, but that is not the subject of this book.

In 1962 the nation rediscovered poverty; in 1963 a new wave of concern about the poor began to sweep across the nation; and in 1964 President Johnson declared unconditional war on this newly rediscovered enemy. In 1964 Congress approved the legislation known as the "Economic Opportunity Act," and the new war on poverty was launched.

This book is about the churches' involvement in that new war. It is written on the assumption that churchmen will be better equipped to respond to the call to enlist in that war if they are informed about the nature of the churches' early participation and the questions that are being raised by that involvement.

Therefore this book has a twofold purpose. The first purpose is to briefly and quickly survey the nature and variety of the churches' participation in this war on an old enemy. The second purpose is to raise up and examine some of the questions, issues, and problems that have emerged from these experiences. It is too early to evaluate the content of the churches' contribution, and therefore very little space is devoted to that question.

The outline of the book reflects these two purposes. The first two chapters describe some of the ways the churches have responded to the call and the way the mobilization has proceeded. Hopefully this will be of interest to churchmen who are now only considering enlisting in the war and to those who seek a progress report on the early months of the war. Experienced veterans may want to skip past these first two chapters.

Chapter 3 presents a description and interpretation of the churches' efforts on the housing front. This appears to be the area in which the interest of the churches is growing most rapidly, and it may attract a larger share of the financial and institutional resources of the denominations than any other front in the war. Various other areas of activity by the churches are reviewed in Chapter 4.

In the next three chapters several of the major questions and issues confronting the churches are examined. Some of these have grown out of the alliances which the churches have entered into, many have emerged from the desire for the "maximum feasible participation" of the poor, and a few have been produced by the lack of clearly defined goals within the churches.

A five-point framework for structuring the response of the churches is suggested in the final brief chapter. This section is based on the assumption that the churches' response should be determined, not by the nature of the immediate problem or by the plea of the government, but rather by the nature of the church and the call of the Lord.

Like all books, this one is the product of many people. It is impossible to list here the names of all the individuals who have contributed to the writing and publication of this volume, but their help is gratefully acknowledged. Several persons, however, were especially helpful in offering advice, information, insights, and ideas or in criticizing a preliminary draft of the manuscript. This list includes Hyman Bookbinder, Milan Brenkus, Richard O. Comfort, John F. Duffy, Jr., Shirley E. Greene, Charles L. Herron, Dean M. Kelley, Donald H. Larsen, Charles Rawlings, Jon M. Templin, A. J. White III, Samuel S. Wiley, Robert L. Wilson, and Paul and Betty Younger.

The reader should not misinterpret this statement and conclude that all these people endorse every statement in this book. Several of them disagree with some of the interpretations and value judgments offered here. These differences of opinion did not inhibit their cooperation, and for this I am grateful. Obviously errors of fact and interpretation are the responsibility of the author and not of generous and helpful friends and fellow churchmen.

This volume is dedicated to the three pastors who helped me find my way into the Christian ministry and to whom I owe a greater debt of gratitude than they realize.

LYLE E. SCHALLER

MAY 30, 1966

CONTENTS

1

Skirmishes and Battles

"We propose to set up child day care centers in locations listed and described below," wrote the Rev. Robert E. Neumeyer. "These churches are strategically located to care for some of our most deprived groups, including Puerto Rican, Negro, and white. We can care for 240 children in these centers, and, if our proposal is approved within the near future, we will begin operation by September."

As he sat in his office on Chestnut Street in the inner city of Philadelphia, sweating over the proposal he was drafting, Bob Neumeyer paused to wonder where this might lead. Here he was as the director of the Center City Lutheran Parish, a cooperative venture tying together twenty-three Lutheran congregations. He already had more work than time in trying to coordinate the work of these parishes, and now he was asking for a $386,000 grant through the Mayor's Anti-Poverty Committee to launch a whole new program. Some of his friends already had questioned whether the churches should get into the war on poverty. There was also the very real question as to the impact this new program might have on the ongoing work of the congregations in the parish. On the other hand Pastor Neumeyer also knew that in Philadelphia there were 122,500 children under the age of twelve with working mothers. He also knew that less than 3 percent of these children were enrolled in approved day care centers.

As he mentally contrasted the need and the resources, he turned back to his typewriter and wrote: "It is becoming increasingly apparent that if we are to make war on poverty, prejudice, and the resulting ills of society, we must utilize every part of the community's resources. The need for child day care centers is evident. The cost of building new facilities is prohibitive. Therefore we of the Lutheran Church in America are offering our physical facilities and leadership resources in order that these children may be helped."

This application for an anti-poverty grant by the Center City Lutheran Parish in Philadelphia was one of the first skirmishes involving the churches in this new war on poverty. Pastor Neumeyer and his colleagues were rebuffed at first, for their request was rejected. In the long run, however, they were victorious. The Board of Education in Philadelphia picked up this idea for child day care and preschool education, which was initiated by the parish and five other agencies, and developed a child care program on a far larger scale under the "Get Set" label.

In this particular skirmish it turned out that the contribution of the churches was far more varied than Bob Neumeyer and his fellow workers had imagined when they first began to think of submitting a formal proposal for a grant from the Office of Economic Opportunity (OEO). First of all, instead of administrators of a program, these churchmen emerged as innovators and stimulators who helped to dramatize and document need and then helped prod an existing public agency into moving ahead in a new direction to meet this need.

Next, the churches had to provide constructive criticism to help keep the anti-poverty effort moving in the right direction.

Third, the churches, after calling attention to a need and arousing community concern, cooperated in recruiting the necessary resources. In this particular battle the Center City Lutheran Parish provided seven church buildings which were used by the Board of Education in the "Get Set" program. As part of this response the Zion Lutheran Church, which was abandoned when the old Swedish congregation dissolved, was taken over by St. Matthew's Lutheran Church as a neighborhood center, and now houses a Get Set program.

Finally, this group of Lutheran churchmen also had to play a reconciling role in helping other churchmen to understand the importance of this effort, to adjust to the resulting inconveniences, and to cope with the bureaucratic red tape which inevitably accompanies such a massive new program.

The experience of Bob Neumeyer and his fellow Lutherans in Philadelphia constitutes only one of the hundreds of battles and skirmishes in which the churches have been engaged in this new war on poverty.

In some of these battles the first shot was not fired until after the President and Congress declared war on poverty with the passage of the Economic Opportunity Act of 1964. In many other cases the battle had been going on for years, and the Economic Opportunity Act simply made additional ammunition available in large quantities.

One of the most notable examples of the churches' involvement in a long-term struggle against poverty can be found in the Mississippi River delta in Missouri's southeastern corner called the "bootheel." Back in the late 1930's the day laborers and sharecroppers encountered hard times, and many families were forced off the land. The Farm Security Administration (FSA) built and operated ten communities, each with from fifty to seventy homes, to house some of these families. In 1945 the FSA decided to sell these properties and the community at Wyatt was sold to commercial interests.

Some churchmen in the area, notably Congregationalists David Burgess and Charles Burger and Episcopal Bishop William Scarlett, recognized that these families might be evicted if the houses were sold to planters or speculators. To prevent that, these three clergymen, with the help of several dedicated laymen, formed the Delmo Housing Corporation, and 550 homes in nine villages were sold by the FSA to the corporation on January 2, 1946, for $285,000. During the next eight years the Corporation carried on a social welfare program and also was able to fulfill the original goal of helping each family buy its own home. In 1954 title to the last house was transferred by the Corporation to a family purchaser. During the next decade the Congregationalists, the Episcopalians, and the Methodists continued the social welfare program which included such diverse efforts as the operation of thrift shops for the distribution of donated

16

clothing, a literacy program for adults, a college scholarship program for young people, and self-help work programs. Throughout its history the Delmo Housing Corporation has sought to enable residents in the bootheel to gain and maintain a sense of dignity and self-respect.

In January, 1965, a new dimension was added to this effort when the Rev. William D. Chapman, an Episcopal clergyman, was called to assist in developing new programs under the Economic Opportunity Act. The program, to be financed in part by a $255,000 OEO grant, calls for a neighborhood service center in each of the nine villages. These centers are intended to offer a variety of services ranging from study centers for both children and adults to medical and dental examinations to training and referral programs for the unemployed and underemployed.

Viewed from a larger perspective the Delmo Housing Corporation has been engaged in a twenty-year war on poverty. This has been more than simply an effort to ease the pain of poverty. It also has been a struggle to enable the residents to break the cycle of poverty in their own family situations. Now, with the new alliance with the federal government, this church-initiated venture has additional resources to pour into the effort.

One of the most important roles of the churches in these early battles and skirmishes has been to act as a critic of the official war on poverty and to serve as a goad in forcing officialdom to take into account the desires and attitudes of the poor. A notable illustration of this is the East Oakland Parish in Oakland, California.

In 1955 Oakland won an award as an "All American City."

Eleven years later it was often described as potentially the most explosive large city in the United States. The combination of racial segregation, inadequate communication, unemployment, poor housing, and poverty had created a tinderbox in the ghetto.

In the midst of this the East Oakland Parish (EOP) was formed in 1964 by pastors and laymen from several churches in the neighborhood. Both Protestant and Roman Catholic congregations are represented, and among the first dozen clergymen to join were two Roman Catholic priests and ministers from eight Protestant denominations—American Baptist, Christian, Church of the Brethren, United Presbyterian, Episcopal, Lutheran Church in America, Methodist, and United Church of Christ. The emphasis has been on "action and people," and one of the major concerns has been the local anti-poverty program.

Basically the parish has taken two approaches to the war on poverty. On the one hand it has launched its own efforts, which include a work-study program employing about thirty students (financed by an OEO grant) who are occupied in community organization and in working with youth groups. In addition, the parish was a prime force in establishing and helping to finance the operation of the John F. Kennedy School, Inc. which is a "school for drop-outs and kick-outs." It has also prepared and submitted proposals for a small business development center and for the construction of a 300-unit low-rent housing project to be financed under Section 221d3 of the Housing Act.

As a part of its second approach to the war EOP has directed a large share of its energies toward influencing the total community battle against poverty. In early 1965, for example, after studying the city's proposal for an anti-poverty grant from OEO, the parish submitted a counterproposal which emphasized the failures of the Inter-Agency Project in reducing unemployment, eliminating the racial imbalance in the public schools, and involving the poor in planning and implementing anti-poverty programs. In its counterproposal the parish submitted a more positive plan for getting at the roots of the poverty issue which emphasized jobs and housing. While the parish failed to gain OEO approval for its program, its aggressive approach has helped move some community leaders in Oakland over to a less conservative position in the war.

In addition to its direct action role, the East Oakland Parish makes a major contribution to the churches' war on poverty in Oakland by acting "as a common meeting ground for determining strategy with respect to the Church's role in confronting and alleviating those social evils which tend to hinder growth in personality and subvert the Christian Gospel from its universal concern for the whole condition of all men as creatures of God." (From Section 6 of Article II of the By-laws.)

Here and there across America individual local churches have launched an attack on poverty without waiting for any direct governmental or denominational assistance. One of the most creative ventures of this type can be found in the Centenary Methodist Church in Memphis, Tennessee. In early 1966 this 725-member Central Jurisdiction congregation decided that every organization in the church should "adopt" a poverty-stricken family. This meant that each organization, including each of the six commissions and each of the circles in the Woman's Society for Christian Service, would fulfill certain responsibilities in relation to its family. Guided by the pastor, The Rev. James M. Lawson, and a special committee chaired by a professional social worker, each participating organization is asked to stay with its family until they have enabled that family to help itself and to lift itself out of the poverty cycle. For example, a circle might provide baby-sitting service for an ADC mother so that she would be free to go to school or to enroll in a job training program.

The two distinctive features of this program at Centenary that make it stand out are (1) the emphasis on *continuing* help and (2) the role of the church as an *enabler*. This is in sharp contrast to the traditional Christmas basket or used clothing collection approach of most local churches in which the effort tends to be a one-shot venture to ease some of the hardships that accompany poverty. At Centenary the thrust is against the disease itself rather than simply relief for the symptoms.

As the churches have responded to the call for a major offensive against poverty, new efforts have been initiated and new coalitions have emerged—sometimes with major subsequent criticism.

An example of this can be seen in North Carolina where in January 1965 the Committee on Ministry to Migrants of the State Council of Churches was invited to meet with the coordinator of the Economic Opportunity Program in North Carolina and with representatives from other governmental agencies concerned with migrants. Since the North Carolina Council of Churches had been providing a ministry to migrant agricultural workers for fifteen years, it was decided that the council was in the best position of any organization represented at the meeting to become the contracting agent. This appeared to be the best way to extend the benefits of the Economic Opportunity Act to the needs of the migrant agricultural workers in the state. Subsequently the council sought and received a $270,444 grant for a program in housing, homemaker services, sanitation, day care for children, and education. This venture was carried on during the summer of 1965 in eight areas covering eighteen counties. It received national acclaim, not only for the quality of the program and the number of persons reached, but also for the meticulous care that was exercised in separating both the financing and the execution of the religious ministry from the balance of the program. Perhaps even more significant was the response from the migrants themselves. They found Christians in North Carolina who cared about them and their plight. They were received and treated as people, their wants and needs were recognized, and they were helped in many ways that would not have been possible without this council-administered anti-poverty program.

What was the result? First, the religious instruction program of the council was inhibited by the extraordinarily careful efforts to keep this separate from the federally financed program, although a full-scale religious program was continued apart from the day-care centers and with funds secured from private sources. Second, some of the financial supporters of the council's ministry to migrants withdrew their support because they concluded the OEO grant made their contributions unnecessary or because they opposed the council's cooperation with the federal anti-poverty program. Finally, the editor of the *Durham Morning Herald* clubbed the council with an editorial stating, "It is a matter of regret that the Council of Churches should compromise the principle of religious liberty by asking [sic] for tax money to finance one of its programs."

In the good old American tradition the critics did not note that the State Council of Churches *was asked* to undertake this anti-poverty program and that in all probability, if the council had refused, the 23,000 migrants working in North Carolina would have been denied the advantages of this program. The critics also ignored the fact that the council was only stepping into a void temporarily until other agencies could take up the work and that the council itself would not receive any financial gain from the relationship.

Despite the buffeting it received from critics in this first skirmish, the North Carolina Council of Churches went right back into the battle in the summer of 1966 as it continued its expanded migrant program with an OEO grant.

Not all churches have responded so vigorously to the strains and stresses of the war. In the District of Columbia a Methodist church backed away from its initial commitment to the Neighborhood Youth Corps when it discovered that this was more than just a means of providing the church with some cheap help and that the church was obligating itself to provide opportunities for job training and cultural enrichment as well as work supervision. In South Carolina a Presbyterian church refused to provide space for an unsegregated Head Start program, although the wife of the pastor had volunteered to direct the program. In Pennsylvania a couple of churches refused to go into a second year of a child service program because of the red tape connected with it. In Delaware three VISTA volunteers approached a Methodist minister and inquired if they could use his church for a tutoring program they were beginning in the community. This minister gave permission to the VISTA girls to use the building, and his action was consistent with the legal definition of his role in The Methodist Church in so doing. When several members of his church discovered that the VISTA workers were tutoring Negro children in the building, they insisted that the permission to use the building be withdrawn, and the VISTA program was evicted.

Other churches which expressed an interest in various programs for children and young people eventually backed away because they were intimidated by the mountains of complicated-looking forms which had to be completed. Several churches have refused to participate because many of the leading laymen were hostile to any form of cooperation with the federal government. In many other churches the requirement that there be no racial discrimination immediately killed any interest that may have existed in cooperating with a federally financed anti-poverty program.

On the other hand a very large but unknown number of congregations have refused to actively cooperate in this new federally financed war on poverty for an entirely different set of reasons. Many churchmen contend that religion is an integral part of all of life, and therefore they will not participate in any program which deprives them of the opportunity to teach and transmit their religious beliefs. They argue that American society is already too secular,

23

and they refuse to take religion out of any part of their ministry.

Others view the federally financed programs as exciting but dangerous detours from their own mission. They fear that active participation in Head Start, the Neighborhood Youth Corps, and similar programs will divert scarce church resources from the primary task of the local church. The desire to maintain their flexibility and mobility has motivated some congregations to reject proposals to become a partner in the local war on poverty. They see how institutional pressures have immobilized many of their sister churches and are anxious to retain their freedom to carry on a prophetic witness unencumbered by institutional, political, programmatic, and financial commitments.

Scores of other skirmishes and battles could be described to demonstrate the churches' commitment to this new war on poverty and to illustrate the many issues and questions that have emerged from experience. Before examining these questions that have produced some major divisions of opinion, however, it may be helpful to first review the manner in which the resources of the churches have been mobilized for this war.

2

The Mobilization of the Churches

For many decades the churches in America have maintained a small standing army which was committed to wage war on poverty. These soldiers have been stationed in both rural and urban communities. The ministry to the migrant workers who harvest a large share of the nation's vegetables is perhaps the most widely known single effort by this standing army, but it is only one illustration. The churches were concerned with the poor in the rural South during Reconstruction and in the urban North when women and children were being exploited by the industrial revolution. The churches fought poverty in the dust bowl during the Great Depression and in Appalachia when the mechanization of mining and agriculture forced men and women of all ages to go on the dole. The churches were there to help the poverty-stricken immigrants from Europe in the late nineteenth and early twentieth centuries. More recently churchmen have been fighting poverty in the cities of the great northern metropolitan centers where the impoverished were left behind unnoticed while the white middle and upper classes rushed to the suburbs with their churches following along behind them.

This standing army included pastors in city slums and in small rural churches. It included teachers and educators in tiny and financially undernourished high schools and colleges all across the South. It included ministers who followed the migratory field hands through the harvesting season. It included workers, both lay and clerical, in settlement houses and missions in the inner city. This army included the house parents and the teachers in over 400 church-related orphanages and children's homes. It also included the uncounted thousands of lay volunteers who gave of their time, their talents, and themselves in staffing these ministries to the poor and the oppressed.

It is easy to overlook the quiet and effective actions of the churches and of this standing army over the years, but it would be more than an oversight to fail to mention these efforts. It would be a false reading of history. Literally thousands and thousands of important programs could be cited to illustrate this long-term and continuing interest of the churches in the plight of the poor. In 1965, for example, Goodwill Industries paid $65,000,000 in wages to the poor who were handicapped. The mission schools of the churches have long been at work eliminating some of the root causes of poverty, both in America and abroad. The churches have helped to resettle literally thousands of refugees from Hungary and Cuba during the past decade.[1]

That is not the purpose of this book, however, and space does not permit an extended discussion of the past efforts of the churches. The focus here is on *new* efforts in this *new* war on poverty which has resulted in a *new* mobilization of national resources, both religious and secular.

Furthermore, it must be acknowledged that while for centuries the churches have been concerned with the problems of the poor, in recent years much of American Protestantism has become institutionally fat and contented and has disengaged itself from the arena where the battles of, on, and for the poor have been fought. During the past thirty-five years the Democratic Party and not the churches of America has taken the initiative in developing and securing the adoption of new legislation intended to help the poor. The labor unions have done more than the churches in directing public attention to the economic problems of the poor *and* in relieving the severity of these problems for millions of American families. Social workers and other members of secular helping professions have been more effective than the clergy in securing the adoption of new enlightened public policies and attitudes at the state and local levels of government. During the three decades from 1933 to 1963,

[1] For a general statement on previous anti-poverty efforts, see Ralph E. Pumphrey, "Past Campaigns in the War on Poverty," *The Social Welfare Forum* (New York: Columbia University Press, 1964), pp. 158-72. For an excellent account of what one denomination has done, see J. Edward Carothers, *Keepers of the Poor* (New York: Joint Commission on Education and Cultivation of the Board of Missions of The Methodist Church, 1966), pp. 119-34.

the contributions of the churches were greatly overshadowed by the efforts of secular agencies in the nation's continuing effort to reduce the severity of the problems created by poverty.

Thus the current effort by the churches to mobilize their resources for an attack on poverty is not a new effort; rather, it represents a renewed interest and enlarged solicitude in a problem that has long been a concern of Christians. The current mobilization is an expression of this renewed interest of the churches and differs from past efforts in four important respects.

First of all, it is an unprecedentedly large-scale effort. During the mid-1960's the churches first began a systematic effort to recruit large quantities of money and manpower for this attack on poverty. Denominational and interdenominational agencies began to allocate significant proportions of their resources to this venture. The local churches have been slower in responding, and thus far only a tiny percentage has begun to mobilize for the war, but they and their resources inevitably will be drawn into the fray, either directly or indirectly.

A second unusual dimension of this war is the degree of cooperation that is present. This degree of cooperation is also without precedent in American church history, and it is manifest in both spirit and action. On the ecclesiastical level this cooperation can be seen in interchurch, interdenominational, and interfaith alliances and coalitions. On the battlefront this cooperation is visible in joint action programs involving religious organizations and either governmental agencies or voluntary social welfare organizations. In the political arena where public policy is hammered out, this cooperation is demonstrated as representatives from four faiths, and many denominations stand shoulder to shoulder in picket lines, in testifying before legislative committees, and in private discussions where the actual political decisions are made.

The third unusual aspect of this mobilization by the churches is that it has been largely a response to external pressures. The earlier efforts by the churches to help the poor were primarily a response to an inner call. Christians responded in the name of Jesus Christ to need. As they sought to live and practice their religion they heeded the injunction of Jesus in Matthew 25:32-45.

Much of the current mobilization, however, is a response to an external call, a call from society in general and the federal government in particular, to join in a great alliance in the war to wipe out poverty in America. While the churches have long been active in fighting poverty in America, the call for this new and vast attack on poverty came not from the churches, but rather from secular sources. In tracing the origins of the current national anti-poverty effort, one of the most astute students of the subject listed three forces behind the current drive—the mounting concern about a rising level of unemployment and the possible effects of automation on unemployment, the Negro revolution, and disarmament. [2] It is significant that while the churches often are mentioned as a major force in the civil rights movement, seldom does

[2] Herman P. Miller, "Major Elements of a Research Program for the Study of Poverty," *The Concept of Poverty* (Washington: Chamber of Commerce of the United States, 1965), p. 118.

anyone suggest that the churches were a major force in focusing national attention on the issue of poverty. The current mobilization by the churches is primarily a response to a secular call to humanize society.

The fourth aspect of this war, perhaps the most important one that sets it apart from earlier church ventures, is the emphasis on the *elimination of poverty*. Historically most of the earlier efforts by both religious and secular agencies have been geared to relieving the suffering that is one of the by-products of poverty. The goal in this war is to wipe out poverty.

This goal requires the input of a much larger quantity of resources. This goal means that the war will last for at least a generation. This goal forces all members of the alliance to think in terms of both immediate objectives and long-range plans. This attack on poverty involves the relief of suffering and deprivation *and* the elimination of the sources and causes of poverty.

Perhaps the most distinctive feature of this mobilization by the churches has been the nonsectarian character of the effort. This can be seen at national, state, and local levels.

National Interfaith

During the first two years following the President's signing of the Economic Opportunity Act, there emerged two significant national interfaith groups.

The more inclusive was the amorphous Inter-Religious Committee Against Poverty (IRCAP), a coalition formed in early 1966 by the National Catholic Welfare Conference, the National Council of Churches, and the Synagogue Council of America.

This committee has urged a greater effort by both governmental and private agencies in the war on poverty and gave a special endorsement to the goal of involving the poor in the planning and execution of the attack on poverty.

Two members of the original committee also served on the National Advisory Council to R. Sargent Shriver and the Office of Economic Opportunity, while five of the leading members of the committee also were active in the Citizens Crusade Against Poverty, a coalition of over 100 organizations which urged greater involvement by private agencies in the OEO programs.

The all-inclusive nature of the IRCAP places some severe limitations on its effectiveness since it must move by consensus and therefore will find it difficult to take an active part in some of the most controversial battles of the war. It can be very effective, however, as a symbol of the churches' concern on a great moral issue, as a platform from which prophetic statements can be issued, as a focal point for coordination of interchurch efforts, as a center for evaluation, and as a lobby to apply pressure on the federal government.

In many respects a more exciting national interfaith venture was the formation of WICS (Women in Community Service). WICS was formed by the National Council of Jewish Women, the National Council of Negro Women, the National Council of Catholic Women, and the United Church Women, to recruit and screen girls for the Job Corps. Later its role was enlarged to conduct special programs for the girls and their families under a $200,000 OEO grant.

31

In its first year 10,000 WICS volunteers worked with the Job Corps in recruiting and screening girls for the residential centers. As the program was expanded to work with the families of Job Corps girls and with other women in poverty, the number of volunteers rose rapidly.

One of the most significant by-products of WICS is that it has placed thousands of women volunteers from middle- and upper-class backgrounds in direct contact with people living in poverty. The importance of this was expressed by an official of WICS in a meeting with Sargent Shriver when she said, "You know, Mr. Shriver, this is not new, we have long been interested in helping girls of this age, but now, for the first time, our women are seeing, meeting, and talking with these girls and their families. Our women will never be the same again."

National and Interdenominational

In addition to these two interfaith ventures the Protestant churches have also sought to mobilize their resources nationally on an interdenominational basis. The most prominent of these ventures centers around the work of the National Council of Churches. In January 1962 the NCC sponsored a consultation on the issue of poverty to stimulate interest among the churches. A report of this conference, "The Churches and Persistent Pockets of Poverty in the U. S. A.," was published and widely circulated, and unquestionably this conference and the subsequent report greatly stimulated the thinking and influenced the activities of many church leaders. Later the Rev. Shirley E. Greene was called to the

NCC staff to coordinate anti-poverty efforts, a unified field staff was developed, and an anti-poverty task force was organized.

The National Council of Churches "encouraged" Professor Henry Clark to write *The Christian Case Against Poverty* (Association Press, 1965) which has been used by study groups across the church in the effort to mobilize interest and concern at the local level.

Thus far the efforts of the National Council have been directed largely to serving as a clearinghouse for information, to encouraging and enabling denominations and local churches to become better acquainted with the challenge of the poverty issue, and to coordinating the work of the churches in the war. Perhaps the major contribution of the NCC thus far has been to help focus attention on the issue and to encourage the development of a large cadre of concerned and informed church members throughout the nation.

The outstanding exception to this generalization is the Delta Ministry in Mississippi. This highly controversial program was begun during the civil rights struggles of 1964 and was sponsored by the National Council of Churches. Gradually the focus of the program has been broadened to include both poverty and civil rights. As the white leaders in the Delta Ministry moved toward an increasingly militant type of action program, white Mississippi Protestants became more strongly opposed to this effort, to the use of denominational funds to finance the program through the National Council of Churches, and, most of all, to the tactics employed by the Delta Ministry. By mid-1966 its support of this one anti-poverty program was beginning to overshadow all the educational and coordinating efforts of the National Council.

As a part of its educational program the National Council also has produced books, pamphlets, filmstrips, and other study materials on the subject of affluence and poverty.

Interfaith and Interdenominational Efforts at the State Level

Some of the most important accomplishments in mobilizing on an interchurch or interfaith basis have occurred at the state level.

The Michigan Council of Churches and the Michigan Catholic Conference joined forces to create Michigan Migrant Opportunity, Inc. This new organization was formed to express the churches' concern for the plight of the migrant workers, and its work has been facilitated by an OEO grant. In Idaho a much more inclusive coalition composed of representatives from the Roman Catholic Diocese of Boise, the State Council of Churches, the Episcopal Diocese, and other farm, civic, and church groups formed the Idaho Farm Workers Services, Inc. to seek an OEO grant "to help migrants and seasoned workers to become economically self-sufficient."

In Mississippi a program called STAR (Systematic Training and Redevelopment) was initiated by the Roman Catholic Diocese of Natchez-Jackson as a nonsectarian, inter-racial corporation with both Catholics and Protestants, and both Caucasians and Negroes, on the Board of Directors. In August 1965, STAR received a $5,300,000 grant from OEO and a $1,600,000 grant from the United States Department of Labor. The central goal of STAR is to enable 25,000

Mississippians now considered to be unemployable to find jobs and become self-supporting citizens.

In North Carolina, Texas, Arizona, New Mexico, Indiana, Ohio, and several other states the state council of churches has served as the focal point for major interchurch efforts in the war on poverty. In New Mexico, for example, the State Council, which includes the Roman Catholic Archdiocese of Santa Fe as a member, secured a $1,360,313 grant in mid-1965 to broaden the scope of its program called HELP (Home Education Livelihood Program). During the first year or two most of these state-wide anti-poverty programs were geared to the problems of migrants, but this emphasis has now been broadened greatly, and several state councils have become involved in job training, literacy programs, and leadership training.

Most of the efforts by state-wide interchurch agencies have been directed toward poverty in rural areas. The war in urban areas largely has been left to denominational or local church agencies and to metropolitan councils of churches.

Mobilization in the Metropolis

The mobilization of the churches' resources in urban areas has taken many different forms and has varied greatly in effectiveness. One of the earliest and most unusual efforts occurred in Cleveland in late 1964 when several denominations, spurred by the Inner City Protestant Parish, agreed to establish the Protestant Ministry to Poverty (PMP) with the Rev. Paul Younger as full-time Director. During the first year of its operation PMP received most of its financial support from five denominations—Presbyterian, Baptist, Methodist, United Church of Christ, and Episcopal. After the old Cleveland Church Federation was reorganized as a Council of Churches (actually a council of denominations) the Poverty agency became a task force in the Council's Commission on Metropolitan Affairs. Both Mr. and Mrs. Younger have been active in many different ventures on the poverty front. These include efforts to increase the welfare payments to an adequate level, recruiting churches to share in Head Start and the Neighborhood Youth Corps, battling for representation of the poor on the local poverty board, helping the poor to organize, and developing the EHOFA proposal (see Chapter 6 for more on this).

The United Church of Christ has been highly visible on the urban front through its Ministers of Metropolitan Mission. In Louisville, for example, where the Rev. William H. Daniels fills this post, the Plymouth Settlement House received $159,722 in an OEO grant to enlarge its program for both children and adults. Daniels also has been a very influential force in helping the poor to gain a voice in planning and administering the war. In Rhode Island the Minister of Metropolitan Mission, the Rev. James S. Caskey, has been very deeply involved and served as a member of the Welfare Committee of Progress for Providence, the local umbrella anti-poverty agency.

In Newark a number of churchmen helped to organize the United Community Corporation in late 1964 which has served as the local clearinghouse for community action requests and grants. The Greater Newark Council of Churches helped to mobilize "grass roots" support for the anti-poverty effort among the churches. When the Newark Pre-School Council needed facilities for carrying out its $2,000,000 anti-poverty program for 4,000 children, Protestant churches provided 30 of the 46 meeting places.

During 1965 and 1966, the greatest contributions by the churches in urban areas were in developing local programs and providing facilities and leadership for the less controversial elements of the war on poverty, such as Head Start and the Neighborhood Youth Corps. Comparatively little attention and energy was devoted to the more difficult and more controversial task of organizing the poor. There were several exceptions to this, however, in cities such as Buffalo, Chicago, Cleveland, Kansas City, New York, Oakland, Rochester, and Syracuse, but even in most of these cities the largest quantity of input by the churches was directed to work with children.

Denominational Contributions

During the first years of this new war the denominational agencies in American Protestantism did comparatively little in mobilizing their resources in support of the war on poverty. This limited effort by the Protestant denominations stands in sharp contrast to the Roman Catholic Church and to the state councils of churches. Both of these have undertaken many new, large-scale anti-poverty programs.

Most of the contributions by the Protestant denominational agencies fall into one of three categories—information and education, allocation of manpower, and financial assistance for local or regional programs.

Several denominations have assisted state or regional judicatories in holding special conferences on poverty and its consequences. For example, in 1965 the Methodist Board of Christian Social Concerns began sponsoring seminars on poverty. Two of the first were held in New Orleans and in Jonesboro, Arkansas.

The denominations have also provided some very helpful study materials for use by churchmen. The November 1963 (note the year) issue of *Social Progress,* a publication of the United Presbyterian Church in the U. S. A., was devoted to the theme "Pockets of Poverty." In September 1965, the Board of Social Ministry of the Lutheran Church in America issued a very thoughtful and provocative analysis of the Economic Opportunity Act and the implications for the church. The May 1, 1965 issue of *Concern,* a magazine of the General Board of Christian Social Concerns of The Methodist Church, was devoted to the church and poverty.

Most of the major denominations have assigned national staff members to give special attention to the war, and several of these persons represent their denominations on the Anti-Poverty Task Force of the National Council of Churches. The denominations also contribute to the financial support of anti-poverty workers out in the field, although most of these men and women were assigned to their present posts as part of the general home missions program of the denominations. While many of them are now devoting much or all of their time to the war on poverty, their jobs were created before war was declared. Only a handful of new positions have been created by the denominations in direct response to the call to mobilize against poverty. Likewise very little money has been appropriated by denominational agencies to be used for new anti-poverty programs involving the churches.

The one major exception to this general pattern of denominational inactivity has been the Board of National Missions of the United Presbyterian Church in the U. S. A. This Board has been very active on the poverty front for several years. It has provided comparatively large sums of money for local efforts in community organization. It has officially directed its staff "to evaluate the use of National Missions money in the light of whether or not it makes a significant response to this challenge and opportunity." In 1965 the Board appropriated $90,000 to be used in the southeastern states to finance the local 10 percent share in nearly a score of anti-poverty programs. Without this outside financial assistance it is doubtful whether the local proposals could have been turned into action programs.

The Influence of the Civil Rights Crisis

Several of the current efforts by the churches to mobilize their resources for the war on poverty originated in the struggle for racial justice in the late 1950's and early 1960's. The Delta Ministry of the National Council of Churches has its roots back in the civil rights movement, but it is more than a struggle for racial equality. It is a comprehensive, long-range, interdenominational effort to improve the economic, social, and health conditions of the poor in Mississippi and is a part of the churches' war on poverty.

In Akron, Ohio, the Protestant Office of Intergroup Relations began in 1963 as an attempt to reduce the barriers of race and culture which have long divided the residents of that city. By early 1966, however, the director was also involved in the churches' efforts to mobilize their resources in the war on poverty.

In Minnesota the interfaith state-wide Commission on Religion and Race, which was organized in the early 1960's as a result of the civil rights crisis, changed its orientation and became an important focal point for mobilizing the churches against poverty.

While it is easy to exaggerate the relationship between the two, there is no question but that in many parts of the nation the churches' involvement in the civil rights movement paved the way for this newer and larger mobilization effort.

An Interpretation of the Pace

At the end of the first two years of the national war on poverty the mobilization had proceeded at a very uneven rate. The most rapid mobilization had occurred in state councils of churches, in areas which had earlier developed an active religion and race commission, in larger parishes and group ministries, in communities where the churches had been operating a social welfare program concerned with a special group of the poor, in the Board of National Missions of the United Presbyterian Church in the U. S. A., and in those local churches which had a direct, immediate, local relationship with a large number of persons living in poverty.

In retrospect it becomes rather easy to explain why this was the pattern of the earliest mobilization efforts.

Nearly all the state councils of churches that moved quickly were those with an active program for migrant workers. In effect they were already mobilized to carry out this phase of the anti-poverty effort, and in many states they were better prepared than any other organization to use OEO funds for a program among migrants.

The change in emphasis from the civil rights movement to the war on poverty was an easy and natural one for most of the persons and agencies who followed this mobilization route. In Cleveland, for example, the Rev. Paul Younger, Director of the newly formed Protestant Ministry to Poverty, had been an active leader in the civil rights movement for several years. When this new anti-poverty agency became a part of the Council of Churches' Commission on Metropolitan Affairs, that relationship with the civil rights movement was continued. The director of the commission is the Rev. Charles Rawlings who had headed the interdenominational Religion and Race Commission in Cleveland from 1963 to 1965.

A quick response to the call also came from most of the churches, parishes, group ministries, and special church-sponsored social welfare programs that had been working closely with the poor. They had a special sensitivity to the problem of poverty, they were organized to combat poverty, and they often had programs in motion that were amenable to a sudden injection of outside resources.

The comparatively high degree of involvement of the Presbyterians as a denomination can be explained in various ways. As one would expect, the religious bodies with a more highly developed and centralized organizational structure would find it easier to mobilize their resources and redirect them to a new cause, such as the war on poverty. Thus it is not surprising to find the United Presbyterians and Roman Catholics moving much more rapidly than the Baptists or the Disciples of Christ. Other closely knit denominations, such as the Methodists, the Episcopalians, and the Lutheran Church-Missouri Synod, have enough unity to move faster than the Baptists and Disciples, but neither group is sufficiently centralized to keep up with the Presbyterians or the Catholics. The Methodist Church is really a federation of annual conferences, the Episcopal Church is a federation of dioceses, and the Lutheran Church-Missouri Synod is a loose confederation of districts held together by a strong sense of doctrinal unity. Thus while an individual conference, district, or diocese may move very rapidly, as a national body each is slowed by important institutional and organizational pressures.

The organizational structure of the rest of American Protestantism bears a much closer resemblance to the Methodists or Baptists than to the Presbyterians, and therefore these other denominations have had difficulty in effecting a rapid mobilization at the state or national level.

A second and perhaps equally important explanation for the rapid pace of the United Presbyterians can be found in the personalities of the leaders of the denomination in general and the Board of National Missions in particular. Several key leadership positions are filled with young aggressive, action-oriented clergymen whose passion for social justice exceeds their concern for custom, precedent, and tradition.

A third factor, which perhaps is related to the first two, is that the United Presbyterian Church, unlike many other denominations, has much of its membership strength in the urbanized northeastern quadrant of the United States, and this makes it easier to develop a consensus for action. The denominations with a large conservative rural constituency find it takes more time to develop a national consensus.

This account is intended only to illustrate some of the many different ways in which the institutional expression of the church has responded to the call to mobilize its resources in the war on poverty. It is not intended to suggest that anything approaching a large-scale mobilization has occurred or even been attempted.

There has been considerable resistance within the churches to the war on poverty, and most of the churches have not joined in the mobilization. In a few instances this refusal has been overt, in most it has been a covert one. Many churchmen contend that the church should concentrate on "religious" issues and leave the war on poverty to secular organizations. Others are ideologically opposed to the whole idea of the war and would prefer to make peace and live with poverty—but not too closely. In the South and border states many churches have either stayed out or dropped out of the war because they did not want to work with Negroes. Perhaps the most common reason for the widespread resistance to participating in the war is indifference and apathy. "There's nothing our church can do." "There are no poor people around here." "The schools and the governmental agencies can do a better job than we could, so let's leave it to them." Comments such as these are heard over and over again in the churches that are still on the sidelines.

The vast majority of the individual congregations in America, most of the denominational agencies, and a large proportion of the councils of churches have yet to commit themselves and their resources to this struggle. Whether they will do so is still doubtful. An increasingly large number of token commitments are being made, but only a very few religious institutions have committed a substantial proportion of their resources to this effort to eliminate poverty in this nation.

The extent of the mobilization of the churches in this new war on poverty in mid-1966 was comparable to the mobilization of the United States for World War II in October 1939, or to the extent of the American involvement in Vietnam in 1960.

In mid-1966, many churchmen still were not sure that this was "our war," and isolationistic sentiments dominated the actions of many of the churches. This lack of commitment to the war can be seen by reviewing the action on the different fronts of the war.

3

The Housing Front

While much of the publicity given to the churches' participation in this new war on poverty has emphasized the alliance with the Office of Economic Opportunity and various community action programs, the churches also have entered the war on other fronts. One of these with the greatest impact is housing.

The Protestant churches of America long have had an interest in housing, but until very recently this was confined to special and very narrowly defined groups of people. Between the close of the Civil War and the beginning of the first World War approximately 400 homes for orphans were founded by Protestant church groups. During the latter part of the nineteenth century and the first half of the twentieth century denominational and local church groups established scores of homes for the elderly. Many of these were founded to "take care of our own," and a large proportion of the residents were retired clergymen and missionaries, their wives and widows and elderly church members. Partially subsidized by the denomination and heavily dependent upon "founders' fees" and bequests, these homes usually had a long waiting list and collectively accounted for only a tiny fraction of the nation's housing inventory. As recently as 1959 all the Protestant church-related homes in the United States combined could offer accommodations for no more than 50,000 persons.

During the latter part of the 1950's and the early 1960's there was a tremendous spurt of interest in church-related homes. This resulted from Congressional approval of three amendments to the Housing Act of 1949.

Section 231 of the Housing Act was adopted in 1959 with the clearly stated purpose, "to help private enterprise to provide housing for the elderly that gets away from institutionalized living." Under the provisions of Section 231, it was possible for nonprofit organizations such as churches to borrow 100 percent of the appraised value of the land and building and to repay this loan over a forty-year period. This easy financing aroused the interest of scores of churchmen, and 170 of the first 282 projects constructed under this law were sponsored by religious organizations. Several of these ran into severe financial difficulties and were turned back to the Federal Housing Administration when the church agency could not keep up the mortgage payments. The vast majority of these projects, however, continued as church-operated homes, and in the first seven years under Section 231 the churches added approximately 20,000 housing units to their inventory of housing for the elderly.

Section 202 of the Housing Act also was adopted in 1959 and was broadened through subsequent amendments. This also proved to be a very attractive program to church organizations interested in housing. It enabled a nonprofit sponsor to borrow directly from the federal government the full amount of the total development cost (land, construction, fixed equipment, fees, etc.) at an interest rate below the market level and to repay this over a 50-year term. About one half of the sponsors using Section 202 in the 1959-1966 period were religious organizations with the Lutherans, Methodists, and Jews leading the way, followed by the Episcopalians, Roman Catholics, United Church of Christ, and Presbyterians.

The third opportunity for the churches to increase their activity in the housing market came with the passage of Section 221d3 which also has been amended several times. This program also offered one hundred percent loans at below market level interest rates and with long term mortgages. Nearly one fourth of the first 400 housing developments to be financed under Section 221d3 were sponsored by churches.

In the seven-year period from 1960 to the end of 1966 the Protestant churches doubled the number of persons that could be accommodated in these church-related homes. Most, but not quite all, of this expansion was facilitated by the financing programs contained in these three sections of the Housing Act. A relatively few church-related homes were built or expanded without any form of governmental financing. [1]

[1] For a more detailed analysis of the churches' role in housing for the elderly, see Lyle E. Schaller, "Church Sponsorship of Housing," *Journal of Housing,* April, 1966, pp. 195-99.

While the housing provided under Sections 202 and 221d3 was for low- and middle-income persons, this should not be misconstrued as suggesting that this was an effort to house poverty-stricken families. First of all, two thirds of the church-related housing was built under Section 231 with rents that usually ranged from $85 to $250 per month. In addition, in many of these new homes a "founder's fee" ranging from $5,000 to $20,000 was required. While occasionally persons of very modest means were accepted as residents, this was and is housing for middle- and upper-income persons.

Housing built under Sections 202 and 221d3 is intended for persons with lower incomes—in Section 202 projects, the income ceilings are $4,000 for a single person and $4,800 for a married couple while Section 221d3 housing is aimed at families in the $4,000 to $10,000 income range. Rents in these projects are usually lower than in Section 231 projects because of the lower interest costs and the longer term amortization of the loan. The difference, however, is seldom more than $20 to $25 per month per apartment. This is not enough to make this housing available to families or individuals with incomes of $1,500 to $3,500 per year.

The Results of These Experiences

While this boom in church-related housing projects did not do much to help persons living below the poverty line, it did produce several important side effects that may influence the churches' contributions to the war on poverty.

First of all, it reawakened the interest of churchmen in active participation in the housing market. This spurt of activity increased the number of churchmen who understand what is involved in opening and operating a church-related housing project. It also stimulated many more churchmen to become interested in housing.

Second, the philosophical question of whether the churches should be engaged in this type of endeavor was debated in a comparatively unclouded atmosphere. The issues in this debate were not obscured by the question of whether the churches should be actively involved in the war on poverty. A consensus did not emerge from this debate, but the majority of the influential opinion molders in the churches appear to have concluded that it is proper for the churches (a) to expand their activity in the housing market, and (b) to use governmental assistance in financing their participation.

Third, the recent experiences of scores of religious organizations has provided an opportunity for churchmen to learn some important lessons from experience. While there is far from universal agreement on the generalizations to be drawn from experience, several points do stand out.

1. A 100 percent loan does not mean that the church sponsor will not have to subsidize the project! Scores of recently constructed church-sponsored housing projects have lost money. Their operating costs exceeded the income from rentals. In some this "loss" was concealed by the fact that gifts, founder's fees, and entrance charges meant that part of the capital expenditures did not have to be amortized. In others, grants from the church sponsor for "administration" offset the operating losses. In several other cases, however,

the loss was more than the church sponsor was able or willing to carry, and the project was turned back to the federal government.

The lesson here is perfectly obvious. Good intentions and a 100 percent mortgage are not acceptable substitutes for a good economic feasibility study.

2. Perhaps the most important lesson that has been learned is the importance of good management. Too often the churches have picked a well-meaning but inexperienced churchman to administer the project. Frequently this has been an expensive mistake. Any interpretation of Christian stewardship emphasizes the need for good management. Even the project which is economically feasible can be turned into a losing-money proposition by poor management. Several well-intentioned but incompetent churchmen have demonstrated the truth of this statement.

3. While a few exceptions stand out, the overwhelming weight of experience strongly suggests that the local church is not the appropriate religious organization for sponsoring a housing project. First of all, such a venture usually diverts a congregation from its primary tasks, weights it down with more institutional baggage than it can comfortably carry, and often creates unexpected demands for time, money, energy, and leadership which produce disrupting tensions within the church.

Second, very few congregations are equipped with the managerial skills and the financial resources necessary for successful execution of such a project. Third, many of the church-sponsored projects now being considered are tied to a forty-year mortgage. How many of these congregations will be in business at the same location for forty years? How many want to commit the next two or three generations of members to the operation of this venture?

Experience clearly demonstrates that a denominational or interdenominational agency, not the local church, is the appropriate organization for operating a church-related housing project.

4. While most of the church-sponsored housing projects have been justified as being constructed for the "needy," in fact only a few of the most needy have been accommodated. The entrance and rental charges in most church-sponsored housing projects have barred the poor and the dispossessed. Very, very few poor people have been accommodated and very, very, very few Negroes have been admitted.

In the past most of the church-sponsored housing has been for white people with incomes above the poverty level. This suggests that new approaches must be found if the churches are to make a major contribution on this front of the war.

5. While the churches have concentrated their efforts largely in the construction of rental housing, there has been enough experience with cooperatives to suggest that this is one of the most attractive alternatives open to churches interested in fighting the poverty war on the housing front. There are various possibilities here, but the most desirable one is for the religious organization to act as a non-profit sponsor. This means that the church group builds the project as a rental operation and then within two years after opening converts it to a cooperative with the tenants constituting the cooperative association. This process enables the church

sponsor to get the housing built where they want it and to get their money out of it so they are able to move on and use these same financial resources to launch another project. The eligibility of cooperatives for rent supplements aid also greatly increases the attractiveness of this approach.

The advantages of the cooperative are many, and most of them grow out of the fact that the tenants are home-owners and not renters. This eliminates some of the social problems such as vandalism that often accompany a rental project, the self-governing process is a constructive feature, management and maintenance costs are reduced, rents are usually about ten percent lower than for equivalent rental units, the turnover rate is about one half that of rental projects, and the monthly charges often can be reduced to the level that poverty families can afford to live there.

Although cooperatives can be built and run at prices poverty families can afford to pay, it must also be recognized that the selection process (down payment of $200 to $500, credit rating check, etc.) tends to restrict this housing to the upper half of the poverty families.

6. Out of the experiences of the churches directly and of other private and public agencies indirectly has emerged a more realistic understanding of the complexity of the housing problem. Some of the early goals have been found to be incompatible. For example, rarely is it possible to provide housing for low-income Negroes in the same neighborhood in which they lived before being displaced by urban renewal or a new freeway *and* to achieve the goal of racial integration. If the housing is designed and constructed to attract Caucasians back into the area it will be too expensive for the

displaced Negro residents. If it is built to stay within the housing budget of the displaced Negro residents, it seldom is sufficiently attractive to draw white occupants. Likewise the churches have found that it is very difficult to build without some form of public subsidy *and* to provide housing for low-income families. Land, construction, and financing costs are simply too high. It also is beginning to be apparent that the frequently articulated goal of persuading religious organizations to invest their endowment funds in housing for the poor will not be achieved. The persons responsible for the investment of such funds are quick to point out that their responsibilities as trustees make it impossible to look favorably upon such high-risk ventures. As *trustees* of investment capital they are neither legally nor morally free to risk the loss of this capital. A major significant exception to this generalization may emerge out of the rent supplements program. While it is too early to justify this on the basis of experience, it does appear that housing operated under the rent supplements program may qualify as low-risk investments for denominational endowment and pension funds.

A fourth result of these efforts by the churches in the housing field can be seen in Washington. The active response of the churches in helping to meet the national demand for housing for the elderly clearly has convinced many officials in the federal government that the churches could be a major resource in providing decent, safe, and sanitary housing for the poor.

Thus when the "rent supplements" amendment to the Housing and Urban Development Act was adopted in late 1965, several governmental officials stated very clearly that they expected the churches would be active in using this provision to provide good housing for low-income families. Their expectations were matched by the reactions of several church leaders who appeared eager to begin some new campaigns on the housing front.

New Campaigns

In looking to the future to see how the churches may fight the war on the housing front, six possibilities stand out most prominently.

The first, and most highly visible, is further enlargement of the housing for the elderly program. This has not, and probably will not, provide much housing for persons living in poverty, but the churches are finding this an attractive outlet for their desire to "do good" and some of the church-related homes do provide accommodations for a few poor people. It is possible that this phase of the program might be enlarged slightly. Even when such a home offers accommodations at below cost, however, the price usually is above what the person living in poverty can afford.

The only significant impact of this program on helping to house the poor is that it does increase the total supply of housing. This in turn has the indirect effect of increasing the quantity of housing available to the poor. While this "trickle down" theory does have a measure of validity, it is something of an exaggeration to suggest that expansion of the current church-related housing for the elderly program will be a major contribution on this front of the war.

The second possibility is that the churches may be stimulated by Medicare to increase their nursing home accommodations. The great need here is for homes that can supply intensive care for the elderly poor. This is an appropriate function for Christian churches, and Medicare may encourage the churches to allocate large quantities of resources to this front. At this writing, however, there is little evidence to suggest this will happen soon.

A third action alternative is for churchmen to realistically recognize that the necessary weapons are not yet available to win the anti-poverty struggle on the housing front. Thus instead of concentrating their efforts on building or rehabilitating housing, the churches would help to define the basic issues and work toward solution of the problems. Instead of expending money and energy on the institutional aspect of the problem, some of these resources could profitably be redirected to strengthening the prophetic voice of the church as it spoke to the political, legislative, and economic issues. Heretofore the churches have been relatively inactive in this area.

Perhaps the appropriate beginning place is to recognize that private enterprise in America cannot provide safe, sanitary, and decent housing for about one fourth of the American population. This means that this housing must be subsidized if it is to be available.

Actually this idea of subsidizing housing for private individuals and families is not a new concept and is already widely practiced, especially for middle- and upper-income persons. For example, hundreds of thousands of college and university students live in tax exempt dormitories which is a form of public subsidy. Relatively few of these dormitory residents come from low-income families. Students from lower-income families tend to live at home in unsubsidized housing while the subsidized dormitories are filled with young people from middle- and upper-income households.

The largest single federal subsidy to housing is the provision in the federal income tax laws which permits home-owners to claim property tax and interest payments as deductions in calculating their income. According to one authoritative estimate, in 1962 this subsidy to the wealthiest one fifth of the American population totalled $1,700,000,000. In the same year the federal subsidy for public housing was slightly less than one half that figure. In other words the federal subsidy for housing for the twenty percent of the American population with the highest incomes was twice the subsidy available to the twenty percent with the lowest incomes. [2]

Whether the form of the subsidy should be in rent supplements, tax abatement, income tax deductions, below-market interest loans, construction subsidies, or a write-down in land costs is of lesser importance. Of greater importance is the necessity of recognizing that some form of subsidy must be provided and that governmental sources must provide all or most of this subsidy. The most that can be expected of the churches is that they may subsidize a relatively few experimental ventures, they can build and operate publicly subsidized projects if this is decided to be preferable to governmental operation, and they can help to change the

[2] Alvin L. Schorr, "National Community and Housing Policy," *The Social Science Review*, XXXIX (December, 1965), 442-43.

climate of public opinion to accelerate the acceptance of the idea of publicly subsidized housing.

At the same time the churches can continue to attack the customs, traditions, prejudices, and laws which intensify the severity of the problem by perpetuating the racial and economic segregation of the population. For example, the provision in the rents supplements legislation which permits local officials to bar this type of housing assistance in their community must be eliminated if this new weapon in the housing battle is to have maximum effectiveness.

While churchmen have been very active in recent years in attacking and reducing racial segregation in housing, much remains to be done. According to one recent study the vast majority of the Negroes in 207 large American cities would have to move if the geographical pattern of the Negro population were to resemble the distribution of white residents. In Chicago, for example, 92.6 percent of the nonwhite residents would have to move to achieve the goal of a nonsegregated city in which each block contained a percentage of nonwhite residents equal to the percentage of nonwhites living in the entire city (based on 1960 data). This percentage figure, referred to by the Taeubers as an "index of residential segregation," would be zero in a completely unsegregated city or in a community where the percentage of nonwhites in each block was exactly equal to the percentage of nonwhites in the total population.

Most cities, however, show a very high degree of residential segregation according to this index. In Philadelphia 87.1 percent of the nonwhite population would have to move to completely eliminate any statistical traces of segregation. In

Cleveland this figure was 91.3 percent, in Atlanta 93.6 percent, in Charlotte 94.3 percent, in Miami 97.9 percent, in Tucson 81.1 percent, in Detroit 84.5 percent, and in Milwaukee 88.1 percent. In many cities, and especially in the South, this index of residential segregation has been rising during the past two decades. [3]

During the past several years many churches have become concerned about this question of residential segregation. They have sought to help establish an "open housing" market in which race would not be a limiting factor. Churches and churchmen have helped to organize "fair housing councils" and similar organizations with a commitment to an open housing market. A survey in 1951 reported the existence of fewer than a score of such organizations; fifteen years later there were over a thousand. Churches have also turned to direct action in helping Negro families find and buy homes in previously all-white neighborhoods.

As a result of these efforts by the churches and other agencies a significant number of Negro families are now able to move into desegregated neighborhoods. While this has not helped the low-income Negro family directly, there has been an indirect effect in that this has reduced the pressure on the housing market in the ghetto.

But still the racial ghetto grows. Despite this escape by a few middle- and upper-income Negro families, the urban ghetto boundaries expand. In most cities the number of Negro families escaping to what have become biracial communities is much smaller than the number of Negroes

[3] Karl E. Taeuber and Alma F. Taeuber, *Negroes In Cities* (Chicago: Aldine Publishing Company, 1965), pp. 28-41.

coming into the ghetto. In Cleveland, for example, while there was a major movement of Negroes to the white eastern suburbs beginning in 1959, two thirds of the increase in the Negro population in the county from 1960 to 1966 had to be housed in the central city.

As churchmen watch this battle against racial discrimination on the housing front it is becoming increasingly apparent to some that simply enabling middle- and upper-income Negro families to find homes in biracial communities is not enough. If the blighting effects of the ghetto are to be eliminated, what began as a battle against racial discrimination in housing must become a war on *both* racial discrimination *and* poverty.

As a result of this growing recognition of the close relationship between these two enemies it appears possible that the churches may shift their emphasis from a battle against racial discrimination in housing to a war on ghetto housing.

This matter of the economic segregation of the population thus stands out as a fourth area in which the churches can make positive contributions. In addition to enabling Negroes to move into previously all-white neighborhoods, the churches should help low-income families, both white and colored, to move out of the economic ghetto in which they are confined by contemporary housing patterns.

The social benefits of breaking down the economic ghetto are obvious. Among other advantages this would provide better educational opportunities for thousands of children who now are not challenged to fulfill their potential, it would reduce the social problems which are multiplied when large numbers of low-income families are concentrated in one area, it would open up new job opportunities for many adults, and it would help millions of middle- and upper-income Americans to become better acquainted with the handicaps of poverty through firsthand observation.

The rent supplements law is one means of accomplishing this goal, although it will not be an effective tool until additional and larger funds are appropriated and until the provision for a local veto is removed. [4] The dispersal of low-rent public-housing dwellings, so that these are scattered throughout the community rather than concentrated to form a low-income island in the central city, is another possibility. The construction of 221d3 housing, both rental and cooperative units, outside the slums is also available as a means of breaking down this economic compartmentalization of the population. [5]

A fifth area in which the churches have begun to be active is in utilizing some of the weapons in the anti-poverty program as a means of reducing the size of the housing problem for the poor. In early 1966 the Office of Economic Opportunity began encouraging local anti-poverty groups to undertake a broad-scale approach in which job development, manpower training, consumer training, community organi-

[4] For a more extended discussion of the rent supplements legislation, see Lyle E. Schaller, "Are Rent Supplements the Answer?" *The Christian Century,* January 12, 1966, pp. 44-47.

[5] For a description of how some churches and civic groups in one urban center have combined for an interfaith and interagency attack on slum housing, see A. Dudley Ward, "Creative Venture in Housing," *The Christian Century,* April 20, 1966, pp. 491-93.

zation, VISTA workers, health and sanitation training, rehabilitation of existing housing, and human renewal could be combined into one comprehensive program.

In such a program low-income persons are encouraged to improve the quality of their housing at the same time they are increasing their own job skills and also learning how to live in an urban environment.

Church groups in Chicago and Cleveland were among the first to explore this new approach. The financing possibilities open under the rent supplements program and under Section 221d3 make this one of the most attractive possibilities for action by the churches. Comprehensive efforts such as these do far more than simply provide shelter; they help the residents acquire new skills, gain a sense of self-fufillment, and exercise a new degree of control over their own lives and their physical environment.

The sixth area of activity by the churches in the housing field is of a different type. Instead of attempting to do the job directly, church-sponsored anti-poverty organizations are being formed to serve as "enablers" and to help others as they become directly involved in improving the housing of low-income families.

On the national level several denominations, including the United Church of Christ, The Methodist Church, and the United Presbyterian Church in the U. S. A., have formed an interdenominational nonprofit housing corporation designed to provide technical, legal, and advisory services to local groups seeking to improve the housing of the poor. In addition, several denominations, including the United Church of Christ, The Methodist Church, the United Presby-

terian Church in the U. S. A., and others, have assigned
staff members direct responsibility for helping state and
local church groups to actively participate in the housing
market.

At the local and regional level interfaith housing committees are being formed to mobilize community resources
for this phase of the war. Such efforts may be directed
toward the recruitment of volunteer services from architects
and contractors who will advise the poor on self-help programs. These local housing committees may concentrate on
raising local capital for a "revolving fund" to finance rehabilitation programs. They may direct their efforts toward establishment of a small staff of experts who can serve as advisors
to neighborhood groups which have decided to undertake a
rehabilitation program. They may put all their energies
behind an effort to encourage existing agencies to increase
their efforts in providing housing for the poor.

While there is considerable activity by the churches in
the field of housing, and the promise of far greater efforts,
it is still too early to tell whether the principal emphasis
will be on direct involvement in a few areas such as housing
for the elderly and nursing homes, or whether the churches
will carry on a wide range of activities in many different
segments of the housing market. The answer to this may be
determined by the extent of the churches' activity on other
fronts of the war.

4

The War on Other Fronts

In discussing this new war on poverty there is a tendency to think of the Office of Economic Opportunity as the headquarters for the federal anti-poverty program. This is fallacious and misleading. While it is true that OEO does administer eleven well-publicized programs, it is also true that many other important components of the total federal effort are housed in other governmental agencies. The Neighborhood Youth Corps is administered by the Department of Labor, the Economic Development program is in the Department of Commerce. The Departments of Agriculture, Justice, Health, Education and Welfare, and Housing and Urban Development also administer major anti-poverty programs. Many of these programs antedate the establishment of OEO. Anyone who attempted to measure the extent of the federal government's participation by studying only the programs of OEO would be overlooking a significant part of the total program.

The same is true in the churches. To presume that the only churches involved in the war on poverty are those with a grant of federal money from OEO or some other governmental agency is fallacious and misleading. As was pointed out earlier in Chapter 2, the church has long maintained a small standing army to fight poverty. While it is impossible to measure these efforts in specific quantitative or qualitative terms, it does appear that most of the churches' contributions to the war on poverty are coming from this small standing army. Their efforts appear to be larger and more important than the new attacks launched by the churches with the aid of federal funds. This is only speculation, of course, and it is impossible to prove such a statement.

In looking at new efforts in this new war on poverty, however, there appears to be little question but that the churches have been stimulated and assisted by *new* federal programs, especially those administered by OEO. These, rather than the continuing programs of that small standing army, constitute the subject of this chapter. Limitations of time and space make it impossible to review *all* the many and varied efforts carried out by the churches in their centuries-long struggle against poverty and the effects of poverty.

In addition to their new level of activity in housing and community action programs which is discussed in general terms in other chapters, the churches also are participating in several other new anti-poverty projects.

VISTA

The churches have been second only to the mass media in making people aware of VISTA (Volunteers In Service To America). VISTA is a program for adult volunteers of all ages in the war on poverty, and by mid-1966, 3,000 individuals had signed up. This total was expected to reach 4,500 by mid-1967.

Unlike the community action programs which are largely directed toward enlarging the staff and program of existing agencies, the VISTA program also seeks to put volunteers into the isolated pockets of poverty and maximize face-to-face contacts. VISTA frequently is described as the "domestic Peace Corps," and there are many parallels between the two. Both programs are based on the idea that thousands of idealistic Americans are looking for the opportunity to "do good" and to help others. Both programs pay the volunteer a subsistence-level stipend. Both programs send back into middle-class communities people who have had a firsthand experience in learning what poverty is and what it does to people.

The churches have helped recruit volunteers for VISTA, they have trained volunteers, and they have supported and are supporting the program in the field. One out of six volunteers first heard about VISTA from the churches. Theological schools such as Princeton Seminary, Union Theological Seminary, and Western Theological Seminary have agreed to accept VISTA as an alternative for the intern year for seminarians. Volunteers in the program have been working in anti-poverty programs sponsored by scores of churches and religious agencies. For example, the New Mexico Council of Churches was assigned 37 volunteers to assist in a state-wide anti-poverty effort. Three settlement houses operated by the United Church of Christ in St. Louis were assigned five VISTA workers to help in tutoring preschoolers and teen-agers and to work in neighborhood development. Eight volunteers were assigned to the Interfaith Migrant Committee of the South Santa Clara Valley in California to fight poverty among the migrant agricultural workers. In Syracuse the Rev. Robert Rowe at Brown Memorial Methodist Church provided a training program for ten volunteers to enable them to acquire skills in organizing people for recreation and other tasks.

This should not be misconstrued as suggesting that the churches have enthusiastically embraced VISTA with open arms and no reservations. Most churches have completely ignored it and several others backed away when they saw the absence of racial segregation in the operation of VISTA. Nevertheless VISTA has provided another opportunity for some churches to share in the war on poverty.

Head Start

The Director of the Office of Economic Opportunity, R. Sargent Shriver, has described Head Start as the most successful of the many federally financed anti-poverty efforts. This offers a variety of enriching educational, health, and welfare services to preschool children from low-income families.[1] During the first summer of operation, Head Start reached 561,000 children in 13,344 centers scattered through 2,398 different communities. In nearly all these centers approximately ninety percent of the cost was borne by grants from OEO. Early evaluations suggested that there not only were significant gains in the intellectual performance level of the children, but also other important benefits. Dr. Julius D. Richmond, Dean of the Medical School of the State University in Syracuse, New York, said,

Even at this early date we can say that gains of the children in widely varying programs have exceeded the expectations of our planning committee. Since the child development centers are comprehensive in nature, we have seen improvement in nutrition and health and vocabularies have shown striking improvements. The children have gained confidence in their relations with people and they are much richer in their understanding of the world about them.

The churches were very active in sponsoring Head Start programs; in fact, Head Start was the area of most frequent

[1] An extremely helpful paper entitled "Guidelines for Churches on Head Start Child Development Programs" has been prepared by the Department of Educational Development in Cooperation with the Anti-Poverty Task Force of the National Council of Churches. This paper describes and evaluates the program and also offers suggestions on the churches' involvement in the program.

For an excellent appraisal of the first year's experience of Head Start, see Edmund W. Gordon, "What Did We Learn?" Julius B. Richmond, "For the Child of Poverty," and S. M. Miller, "Strategy for Change," *American Child,* Spring, 1966, pp. 5-24. For a helpful account of the experience in one of the first programs, see Kathryn G. Morgenthau, "Reflections on One Head Start Program," *International Journal of Religious Education,* May, 1966, pp. 17, 48.

participation by the churches in the new war on poverty. Nearly a hundred separate child development programs were sponsored by the churches that first summer. Some of these were relatively small with a single church serving as sponsor while others were very extensive with a council of churches, a diocese, a church school, an interfaith committee or an ad hoc group serving as the sponsor. Many other churches shared in Head Start by working with a secular sponsor.

While educational leaders, professional churchmen, and social workers expressed great enthusiasm for Head Start, there are problems in it for the churches. The church-state question troubles many while others wonder how the churches will fulfill the responsibilities they appear to be assuming. For example the health program of Head Start found that nearly one third of the children had major physical defects while two thirds had extensive dental problems. In the church-sponsored programs, will the churches be able to see to it that these health problems are corrected? Or should they expect some other agency to assume this responsibility?

In its second year of operation, Head Start ran into serious financial problems. The demand exceeded the funds available. The actual funding of some programs was so late in coming that it became very difficult to secure competent staff to direct the centers. The program for the summer of 1966 was cut back by 60,000 children to the 500,000 level, but it was expected to move back toward 600,000 for the summer of 1967. In addition, funds were sought for year-round Head Start centers for 100,000 children in 1966-67 and 200,000 in 1967-68.

This raises a financial and moral question for the churches. Head Start is an experimental program. It costs about $100 per month per child. In view of the need and the shortage of federal funds, should the churches offer Head Start programs without federal aid? The churches were quick to respond when ninety percent of the cost was met by OEO grants. If the federal share drops to fifty or seventy percent, will the churches be as quick to participate? Is Head Start a good program for the churches to share in? Or is it a good program for the churches only when the federal government is paying ninety percent of the cost?

Head Start focused attention not only on the needs of children, but in literally hundreds of cases it also focused attention on the physical condition of the buildings housing this special program. Many congregations willingly gave official permission for their building to be used for child development centers. After all, it would not cost the congregation anything, the local sponsor could get credit for the value of the rent toward the required local contribution, and the members of the church could gain satisfaction from this "outreach to the neighborhood."

This was about the way it worked in 1965 when everyone was in a hurry to get the program under way. By 1966, however, local officials were enforcing the building regulations and requiring code compliance in the churches in which the program was to be housed. For many congregations this meant a sudden and unexpected investment of scarce resources to install restrooms, add or rebuild exits, replace dangerous electrical wiring, and make other repairs necessary for compliance with public safety requirements. Because of the nature of the program it was usually the oldest buildings and the poorest congregations in the neighborhoods with least resources that were confronted with these unanticipated financial demands. In at least a couple of cases the continued life of the congregation was jeopardized because of the cost of suddenly being required to bring their building up to code standards.

In several communities the churches have been competing with the public schools and with private voluntary agencies for money for Head Start programs. Should the churches seek to participate in a program such as this when the capacity of public and private agencies is sufficient for the task? Should the churches strive to do the job? Or to see that the job is done competently?

One of the unforeseen results of Head Start is that in some communities it has produced a shortage of children for summer programs. The churches, the settlement houses, and similar agencies have been increasing their summer programs for underprivileged children. Suddenly Head Start and other programs directed toward poverty children came along and took a half million youngsters "out of the market" for six to eight weeks with better and more enriching programs. Some programs were canceled and others were rescheduled. Many were conducted with a middle-class clientele—thus eliminating the goal of providing an opportunity for children from varying economic and cultural backgrounds to become acquainted.

While many questions about the churches' participation in Head Start remain unanswered, there is little reason to

believe that these questions will reduce the churches' interest—
as long as the ninety percent subsidy is available.

Migrant Programs

One of the most important and long-established anti-poverty
programs of the churches has been the effort to work with
migrant agricultural workers. These programs were in existence many years before America "rediscovered" poverty.
The new war on poverty provided the opportunity to
mobilize additional resources for this work.

An outstanding illustration of how the new war on
poverty stimulated the churches' efforts on behalf of the
migrant farm laborer can be seen in Indiana. In 1940 the
Migrant Ministry of the Indiana Council of Churches was
established to help assist the migrants. Ten years later the
Migrant Apostolate of the Catholic Dioceses of Indiana was
founded. In 1959 the Indiana Citizen's Committee on Migrant
Labor was formed to encourage legislation on behalf of the
migrant worker. In late 1964 representatives from the State
Council of Churches and from the Migrant Apostolate began
meeting and discussed the formation of a group to plan,
initiate, and coordinate efforts in this field. Subsequently
representatives from other interested agencies shared in these
discussions and AMOS was born in January 1965, and
incorporated in February 1965. AMOS is an acronym for
Associated Migrant Opportunity Services, Inc.

A grant of $484,704 was secured from OEO to finance the
first year of operation of AMOS. A fifteen-project program
was launched to serve migrant families in ten Indiana

counties. A total of 1,556 migrants were directly served in 1965 by this program which included five remedial schools, two community centers, three day care centers, one day camp, a state-wide literacy program, a social education unit, an adult education program, and a state administrative unit. This program cost $231,941 in 1965 with over forty percent being spent on remedial education while another twelve percent was allocated to adult education.

While AMOS placed a major emphasis on education and self-help in its first year, it is also concerned with the elimination of child labor abuses, improvement of housing for migrants, more adequate wage levels, and the eventual goal of a year-round stabilized work force.

During its second year of operation AMOS expanded and improved on its initial year of success. It broadened its scope of services to include additional counties and more comprehensive services. The expansion enabled AMOS to directly serve 4,000 to 5,000 migrants with the broad and varied program which included eight remedial schools, two opportunity centers, eighteen child care education and service centers, a social education program, a traveling migrant teaching team, and an expanded program for the Advancement of Capabilities in adult education, a state-wide literacy project, state conferences in the areas of teacher training, and a state administrative unit. During its second year of operation AMOS increased its efforts in the areas of migrant education, self-help ability development, and housing and sanitation.

In essence, the AMOS programs are designed to help the Indiana migrant help himself defeat poverty and human degradation. AMOS seeks to cooperatively build a foundation

72

on which the migrant can build a life where his basic physiological needs are met, his safety and security are protected, his esteem and self-respect are enhanced, and through which he has an opportunity for self-realization.

Just as AMOS offers new hope to thousands of migrant agricultural workers in Indiana, similar programs sponsored by the churches in other states are directed to this phase of the war on poverty.

It is very possible that this ministry to migrants is the churches' greatest single contribution to the war on poverty. There is no question but that the churches' contribution to this phase of the war effort looms larger by comparison with secular efforts than that on any other battle front.

Job Training

When compared to their contributions on behalf of the migrants, the churches' efforts in job training appear very meager. While it is possible to point to a few spectacular individual efforts such as the retaining program sparked by the Rev. Leon Sullivan in Philadelphia, these are the exceptions and usually are the product of a single charismatic leader rather than the result of a systematic program by the churches. [2]

The largest single contribution by the churches to this phase of the war is in the Neighborhood Youth Corps.

[2] For a description of this pioneering effort, see Leon H. Sullivan, "Doors Open in Philadelphia," *International Journal of Religious Education,* May, 1966, pp. 20-21, 46. See also the *American Child,* Winter, 1966, for an analysis of the first year's contributions of the Job Corps.

Scores of churches have participated in this venture and have provided work experience training for young persons. The program is geared to the sixteen- to twenty-one-year-old person and offers either part-time employment which will enable the individual to remain in school or full-time employment to help him improve the skills he is offering on the labor market.

A few religious organizations have entered directly into job training programs, but these tend to be the exception. Only a few church groups are organized in a manner to enable them to do this. A few churches have been active in recruiting candidates for the Job Corps, and the interfaith Women in Community Service (WICS) has been especially helpful in recruiting and screening young women.

An example of how the churches have participated directly in job training is Project Peace Skills Center in Cleveland. Sponsored by the Catholic Board of Education, Catholic Charities, and the Catholic Interracial Council, this anti-poverty venture received an $800,000 grant from the United States Department of Labor and the Department of Health, Education, and Welfare to train persons with limited educational and employment backgrounds. Basically this is an experimental attempt to train unemployed and underemployed adults so they may compete successfully in the contemporary employment market.

One of the places where little has been heard from the churches is in the Job Corps. This program, which bears a resemblance to the Civilian Conservation Corps of the 1930's, resulted in the opening of 87 training centers by early 1966. A young adult who enrolls in this program leaves home and goes to one of these centers where the program is geared to upgrade his health, his education, and his employment skills. While the nature and scale of this program precludes direct church participation, some observers expected that local churches would encourage the people in their communities to endorse the establishment of a Job Corps Center and would provide a welcome for the trainees. While it is true that a few churches have done this, most have been silent and inactive, while community leaders opposed the creation of the proposed center and the newly-arrived trainees were treated as outcasts. Most of this opposition to the centers and rejection of the trainees reflect racial and economic prejudice. The teachings of the churches appear to have been ineffectual in overcoming this prejudice.

The Rural Front

Perhaps the greatest opportunity for the churches to make a large and distinctive contribution to the war on poverty is in rural America. Nearly one half of the poor live in rural communities. Most of the public and private voluntary agencies that have the necessary institutional strength to wage war on poverty are located in urban areas. In metropolitan centers the churches constitute only one of many organizations that can be mobilized for this new war. By contrast in rural areas there is a comparative scarcity of institutionally strong social welfare agencies, and the local church stands out as one of the few organizations which can be an effective ally in this new war.

For example, the new Rural Community Development

Service in the Department of Agriculture is intended (1) to help rural residents gain a voice in the administration of services to rural areas, (2) to enable sparsely populated areas to obtain a full range of services, and (3) to make OEO grants more readily available to rural areas. The churches in rural America can help to achieve both these general goals and more specific goals developed by local residents.

As mentioned earlier, the churches have been very active in helping to alleviate poverty and the effects of poverty among migrant agricultural workers. Hundreds of churches also have participated directly and indirectly in community development programs and in OEO programs such as Head Start for rural residents.

Attacking poverty in rural areas is a very difficult task, however, and it is too early to predict how the war will go on that front. While poverty is more common in rural areas than in urban centers, it it is more scattered and therefore more difficult to treat. This, coupled with the lack of resources and the distinctive role of the church in rural America, make both the challenge and the opportunity one of the greatest that confronts the churches.

Other new ventures of the churches, such as the tutorial programs, family planning clinics, and adult education classes, merit mention for they are significant. However they tend to represent the efforts of individual churchmen rather than of the institutional church and thus are somewhat outside the scope of this chapter. Many of these ventures, as well as others described earlier, also represent alliances with secular agencies, and it may be more helpful now to examine some of the tensions produced by these alliances.

5

Uneasy Alliances

When the full-scale war on poverty was launched in 1964, there was an immediate rush to develop alliances among those who sought to vanquish poverty. In several respects these diverse efforts to forge alliances and coalitions paralleled the processes that went on in Europe before World War I and before World War II. Another parallel can be seen every four years in the United States as candidates for the presidential nomination set out to form broad-based coalitions to support their political ambitions.

As the major power in this war, the federal government has been vigorously courting allies to help it achieve victory. It should also be recognized that, as the federal government brings partners into this alliance, it not only increases the strength of the alliance, it also reduces the size and strength of the potential opposition. As this alliance becomes larger and more inclusive, the number of potential critics and opponents is reduced.

The federal government has been successful in courting and winning a great number and variety of allies—labor unions, public school systems, municipal governments, voluntary welfare agencies, large commercial and industrial corporations, colleges and universities, journalists, public relations specialists, key political leaders, and the churches. The size and strength of these alliances is one of the major political phenomena of the decade. The speed with which they have been built and the national consensus that has been created have awed many political observers. Much of the credit for this achievement must be given to the political skill of two men—Lyndon B. Johnson and R. Sargent Shriver. Another important factor, however, has been that the federal government has been eager to share the resources in its arsenal with its allies. There was money to be allocated, patronage to be dispensed, and dreams to be fulfilled. Many of the new allies quickly saw that here was an opportunity that would enable them to enlarge their own programs, accelerate their rate of progress, and strengthen their own institutional position.

At the same time the churches were entering into alliances with the federal government, they also were out to strengthen old alliances of their own and to build new ones. As a result the Protestant churches today find themselves involved in a massive and complex attack on poverty. As a part of this effort the churches have entered into new, or strengthened old, alliances not only with the federal government but also with a variety of other groups. There are interdenominational and interfaith alliances. There are alliances between the churches and the civil rights movement, between the churches and agencies that only yesterday were attacked by the civil rights movement. There are alliances between the churches and the power centers of the community, between the churches and the powerless. There are alliances between those in the church who have borne the label "activist" or "radical" and those who identified themselves as "moderates" or "conservatives." The churches are involved in alliances beyond count and beyond description.

One of the most significant by-products of the churches' war on poverty has been the tensions produced by this burgeoning multitude of alliances. Collectively they represent a major diversion from the task itself as the churches participate in the war on poverty.

The Church-State Issue

Unquestionably the uneasiest of all the alliances the churches have entered is the one with the federal government in general and the Office of Economic Opportunity in particular. Many churchmen who have been fighting to preserve the spirit of the First Amendment to the Constitution and to strengthen Thomas Jefferson's "wall of separation between church and state" are greatly disturbed by this alliance between the federal government and the churches in the war on poverty.

Some of these critics feel that once the pattern of separation is broken the churches may try to dominate the government and the government may try to control the churches. Others see the anti-poverty program as a part of a plot by the Roman Catholics to secure federal aid for parochial schools.

On the other hand many of the churchmen most active in the war seem completely untroubled by this issue. As one of them said, "The people who appear most concerned about the church-state issue are the ones the farthest from the action. Most of us who are on the firing line are overwhelmed by the magnitude of the job to be done, and our prime concern is to rally all the resources we can for the battle. This includes both the Catholics and the federal government."

The use of religious buildings for federally financed anti-poverty programs has been an especially sore point. In Kansas City the Methodist Inner City Parish asked the public school system to assume responsibility for future Head Start classes, thus eliminating the need for using church buildings. Protestants And Others United (PAOU) initiated suit in a Jackson County, Missouri court challenging the constitutionality of participation by the Roman Catholic Diocese of Kansas City–St. Joseph in the Head Start program. This suit was dropped when the public schools agreed to operate the Head Start program.

The basic rule that Head Start and similar programs for children can use church rooms only where there are no religious symbols displayed or where these symbols have been removed appears to be aimed primarily at Roman Catholic participation. In fact it has been much more difficult to enforce this in Protestant churches than in Catholic buildings. In several poverty-stricken inner city neighborhoods, for example, the storefront church is the best channel for reaching the residents of the neighborhood. Since these are usually one-room churches, it is unrealistic to expect the program to be carried on in a room where there are no religious symbols.

Another related criticism has been that perhaps OEO did not completely explore *all* other avenues before going to the churches for the use of their facilities. This is a very subjective question and it is difficult to give an adequate answer when the pressures of time versus the problems of bureaucratic indecision are weighed.

When the old "child-benefit" doctrine was resurrected in the passage of the Elementary and Secondary Education Act of 1965, another door was opened whereby the government could wage war on poverty via the programs of religious organizations. In effect this doctrine states that public funds may be appropriated for facilitating the operation of privately operated programs if the money is expended for the benefit of the child rather than for the benefit of the sponsoring organization. The immediate application of this doctrine was in providing public funds for textbooks and for the transportation of children enrolled in private schools. The same doctrine, however, could be used to justify financing a variety of church-sponsored programs intended to aid the child living in poverty. [1]

With several notable exceptions, Protestants have generally agreed that while the church-state issue is important, it does not constitute an insurmountable barrier to the alliance between the federal government and the churches in this war. A typical decision is that of the Maryland Synod of

[1] For an attack on the constitutional validity of the "child-benefit" doctrine, see Leo Pfeffer, "The Child-Benefit Theory and Church-State Separation," *Church & State,* April, 1966, pp. 6-15.

the Lutheran Church in America which in the spring of 1965 approved a resolution which declared that "where feasible, synod's congregations, agencies, and combinations thereof, institute proposals and engage both urgency and discretion in approved programs, government-sponsored or other, for the alleviation of social and economic ills of people due to or related to poverty."

Defenders of this awkwardly-worded resolution argued that the separation of church and state in America is not absolute and that "the church cannot be blind to the poverty in our land today. The church must be relevant and speak to the needs of man."

Throughout the churches one can hear similar arguments on behalf of this alliance. Churchmen argue that the problem of people in "desperate need" is more basic than the church-state question, that the size of the task and the scarcity of resources require the church to take advantage of every available opportunity for help, and that the lack of far-sighted leaders who "really understand" the plight of the poor requires the church to take the lead. Others contend that, since government is oriented to problem-solving and is not primarily motivated by ideological considerations, there is little danger that governmental actions will be influenced by any religious philosophy.

In a devastating response to these kinds of arguments Dean M. Kelley of the Department of Religious Liberty of the National Council of Churches has warned that church-men may be overlooking the unique contribution the church does have to offer in the healing power of the Word. Kelley suggests that in their hurry "to get into the act too" with social services, churchmen may be "withholding the very ingredient without which the rest may very well not hold together!" He warns that "government is always eager to maximize its channels of access to the people and its networks of support among them, and the churches offer an ideal public in both respects. But the churches must not become advance men for the government, lest they lose credibility and their independence." Kelley goes on to suggest that perhaps now, when secular agencies are moving into social service and educational programs on a large scale, the time has come for the churches to get out of these functions and concentrate on their *unique* role and unique contributions.[2]

Kelley, Wayne Hartmire, and others have warned that the Economic Opportunity Act may be a diversion from what could and should be the churches' most meaningful attack on poverty and its root causes. They offer a very persuasive argument that by becoming sub-contractors for the federal government the churches may be diverting themselves from this task. The churches must remain free, not only for the uninhibited preaching of the Word, but also free to engage in the appropriate forms of social action necessary for expressing and communicating the gospel. When the churches become an agent for a secular institution, this freedom is inhibited.

This does not mean that the churches should remove themselves from the struggle, but that the churches should be there reenacting the crucifixion rather than masquerading as welfare workers.

[2] Dean M. Kelley, "The Church and the Poverty Program," *The Christian Century,* June 8, 1966, pp. 741-44.

In addition to the general question of separation of church and state, there are other dimensions to this alliance that worry some churchmen.

There can be no question but that the availability of federal funds has affected the program priorities for many religious organizations. The most obvious illustration of this is the Head Start project and similar programs for children and young people. Churches and councils of churches that had absolutely no idea of becoming involved in such activities suddenly found themselves in 1965 and 1966 downgrading the priority of some of their other responsibilities in order to participate in these anti-poverty programs. On a smaller scale the same shifting of priorities occurred as churches saw the chance to obtain federal funds for an expansion of their work with migrants, to participate in the work-study, retraining, literacy, and community organization programs.

This is not a criticism of these programs nor of the use of federal funds. It does raise the very fundamental question, however, "Who is setting the program priorities for the churches?" The churches? The federal government? The new alliance?

Another source of uneasiness is that when the churches entered into this alliance they surrendered part of their freedom to speak with a prophetic voice. Can the church *freely* criticize the ally who is supplying ninety percent of the resources for the war? Any realist will recognize that by entering into this alliance the churches have surrendered part of their freedom to speak with a prophetic and critical voice to the policies and actions of the government. The extreme critics even argue that the church has been "bought off."

Whether the churches have traded control over the setting of priorities for a piece of the anti-poverty fund is a debatable issue. There is no question, however, that active cooperation in program planning and execution does drain off energy and use up time that might have been devoted to a critical evaluation of the program, to promoting greater participation by the poor, or to strengthening the civil rights movement.

Is the Church a Natural Ally?

While seldom anyone openly raises this issue, one of the reasons for the uneasiness about some of these alliances is that many churchmen have grave doubts about whether the churches should be involved in this war. Even a quick look at church history supplies plenty of grounds for these doubts. During the industrial revolution the Protestant ethic supported the belief that success was a sign of godliness, poverty a sign of shiftlessness, and that poverty was a harmonious element in God's plan for creation. During the rest of the nineteenth century, Protestantism continued to regard poverty as a natural result of the sinfulness of the individual. Even the efforts of the reformers were directed to crusades against drinking and vice rather than against the causes of poverty.

By 1900, most main-line Protestant churches had become entrenched allies and supporters of the middle and upper classes. As the nation moved into the second half of the twentieth century, critics were speaking of the "suburban captivity of the churches" and most of the main-line Protestant churches had disappeared from the neighborhoods where the poor lived. The Protestant churches, for the most part, had become solid, conservative, middle-class institutions with a middle-class set of priorities and a strong emphasis on serving the members of the congregation, rather than on evangelism or social action.

Thus for many conservative laymen there was good cause for questioning whether the church had any business getting mixed up in the war on poverty. These people look, from their perspective, at the history of American Protestantism and can see no reason why their church should enter into any alliance to effect social change, whether it be by fighting poverty or helping the poor to organize to help themselves.

Those who contend the churches should be in the war can marshal a much more impressive array of arguments to support their position. These range from the New Testament to the churches' missionary programs in foreign lands, from the prophets of the Old Testament to the churches' share in the civil rights movements, and from the teachings of Jesus to the new inner city ministries established in the 1890's or the 1950's.

This is not the point, however. Those who question the churches' involvement will not be persuaded by proof texts. Those who believe the church should be a haven of security from change and the threat of change will not be swayed by a few isolated illustrations of how the churches have helped achieve social justice.

Conservative churchmen were not the only ones, however, to raise serious questions about the propriety of the churches becoming a partner in this alliance. As was pointed out earlier, laymen and ministers at the other end of the political spectrum often viewed this as a war on the poor. Some of these churchmen argued that if the churches joined the alliance they would be helping to perpetuate the system which is a basic cause of poverty. These churchmen contend the churches must stay out of the alliance in order to be free to fulfill their prophetic role.

The result is that while those outside the church see the churches as natural allies with much to contribute to the war effort, a great many church members have grave reservations about the war itself and even more reservations about whether the churches should be active allies. This division of opinion naturally reduces the contributions the churches can make to the alliance.

From the perspective of a federal official a very logical way to prosecute the war on the many local fronts would be to develop community-wide coalitions of like-minded people and agencies with similar goals. The creation of these local coalitions would facilitate both the decentralization of the total program and the coordination of local efforts. [3]

A logical method of implementing this would be to urge or require creation of one central clearinghouse-type organization which would receive all requests for federal anti-poverty grants and which would also be able to coordinate local efforts. Presumably the major participants at the local level would be the governmental agencies (municipalities, county government, and boards of education), the private

[3] For an excellent explanation of why this is the natural position of officials out to wage war on poverty and of the shortcomings of this position, see Edgar S. Cahn and Jean C. Cahn, "The War on Poverty: A Civilian Perspective," *The Yale Law Journal*, July, 1964, pp. 1317-52.

voluntary health and welfare agencies (welfare council, settlement houses, neighborhood centers), and the churches. Here,
it appeared, was the basis for a natural alliance of agencies
with similar goals and purposes that could carry the war to
the local level.

In dozens of communities this alliance has been formed
and is carrying on the fight against poverty.

In many other communities, however, it has been much
more difficult to form an effective coalition along these
lines. The obstacles have been far greater than was anticipated.
First of all, it was very quickly apparent to every astute
politician that the war meant the creation of new jobs and
new resources. Who would control the allocation of these
resources? The public official reasoned that since these were
public funds that were to be spent, the majority of the control
should be placed in the hands of public officials. The
professional social worker reasoned that, since this was basically a social welfare program and since the private welfare
agencies had *both* experience in the field *and* freedom from
political pressures, the voluntary welfare agencies should
have a major voice in the allocation of anti-poverty funds.

Many of the churchmen who first took an interest in the
war on poverty were individuals who had been active in
the civil rights movement of the late 1950's and early 1960's.
They saw a coalition being formed to administer the local
anti-poverty program which looked suspiciously like the
"enemy" they had been fighting in the civil rights struggle.
Only recently these same church leaders had been in conflict
with public officials over de facto segregation in the public
schools. They had testified on allegations of police brutality in

the arrest of Negroes at sit-ins and on the picket lines. They had struggled valiantly, and often fruitlessly, with public officials to secure enactment of fair housing laws. They had protested the "welfare colonialism" which deprived the recipient of his dignity as he sought public assistance. They had been defeated in the efforts to raise the scale of public assistance payments to a subsistence level.

Now these same churchmen who were accepting leadership in the churches' war on poverty were being asked to join their former opponents in a new coalition. These churchmen, who had identified themselves as allies of the powerless, were now being asked to join a coalition composed of the holders of power. Some churchmen refused on the ground of incompatibility. They felt that they could not be allies of the powerless and the powerful at the same time, and they believed the churches could not abandon their new alliance with the powerless. Others accepted for a variety of reasons, but often with great uneasiness. At best it produced an uneasy alliance, and in many cities it resulted in a relationship ranging from conflict to a temporary truce.

The weaknesses of this alliance also appeared when specific anti-poverty programs were being developed. The public schools saw this as an opportunity to enlarge and enrich their offerings. The private, voluntary welfare agencies saw this as a chance to increase the range of their services—furthermore if they did not do this they might soon be out of business. They might be so overshadowed by this massive effort financed with public funds that they would lose their visibility—and therefore the basis for their appeal for private funds. The churches and religious agencies saw this as an opportunity to extend their program—and also to strengthen their justification for existence.

The result has been competition for power, prestige, and programs within the alliance.

While some of the local alliances have produced a smoothly functioning local agency, in others the simple effort to create the alliance has accentuated the differences which divide the opponents of poverty and has dramatized the lack of any common purpose or goal. These great differences in goals, which are discussed in more detail in a later chapter, make it unreasonable to believe that a strong unified local alliance can be formed from these groups until there is greater agreement on goals.

It is also significant that the alliance between the churches and the private volunteer secular social welfare agencies which had flourished for decades has been seriously weakened by conflicts growing out of the war on poverty. In some metropolitan centers the old alliance was broken up when the churches took a more militant position on civil rights and the participation of the poor. In others the alliance was threatened because of open competition between the churches and the private voluntary agencies for power, for places on the local poverty board, for program grants, and for preservation and enlargement of their respective empires.

Perhaps the most fundamental threat to this alliance came in those communities where the voluntary welfare agencies viewed the new war on poverty as merely the continuation and expansion of old welfare service programs. By contrast some of the churches took an entirely different view. Instead of viewing it as a service-oriented operation, these churches saw this as a means of enabling the poor to have a voice in diagnosing the problem and prescribing the solutions. They saw this as the beginning of a change in the relationship between the poor and those who served the poor. This is not to suggest that all churches took such an enlightened view nor that all social welfare workers failed to recognize this new theme. There were, however, enough professional social welfare administrators functioning in the traditional manner and enough churchmen who saw the vision inherent in the concept of maximum feasible participation to create tensions which threatened the alliance between the voluntary welfare agencies and the churches.

Interfaith and Interdenominational Alliances

In the early days of the war there were some observers who viewed the efforts to create interfaith and interdenominational alliances with great skepticism. They felt that the differences among the faiths on such questions as federal aid to religious organizations and the proper role of the church in social action would make it impossible to create any meaningful interfaith alliances. Similarly some felt that the weaknesses of interdenominational cooperation would limit interchurch efforts in the war on poverty.

While it is too early to make any definitive analysis, it now appears that these alliances may be sturdier than was once believed possible. In the first years of the war interdenominational efforts overshadowed denominational programs in both quantity and quality. In part this was because interdenominational agencies were ready to move quickly. The work of the state councils of churches with migrant farm labor is an outstanding illustration. In part this was because the denominational agencies, for institutional, theological, and political reasons, moved very slowly. Even a minor interchurch effort loomed large in comparison with what most denominational and local church agencies were doing.

There was also a natural selective process at work which meant that most of the decision makers in the interdenominational agency shared a common point of view on ecumenical relations and on social action. If they did not hold this viewpoint, they probably would not have been there.

By contrast most local church and denominational agencies have a more heterogeneous assortment of viewpoints in leadership posts. It takes longer to build the consensus necessary to launch a major program in a new area such as the war on poverty.

Thus the interfaith and interdenominational agencies have had a somewhat freer hand to ignore those churchmen who have reservations about the churches getting involved in this effort. Perhaps the outstanding illustration of how an interdenominational effort can offer a wide degree of freedom for the participants is the Delta Ministry in Mississippi. An agency of the National Council of Churches, the Delta Ministry has been able to function in a broad variety of areas because it has been free of many of the restraining influences that would be inherent in a denominational venture of this type.

While some of the alliances into which the churches have been entering have been relatively peaceful and productive, there is no reason to believe that all the many alliances will become stable and harmonious relationships. Whenever and wherever the churches enter into an alliance to affect the course of social change, it is inevitable that certain traditions, standards, and values will be threatened and that some churchmen will become extremely uneasy because of these threats to established patterns. This is a part of the price the churches must pay for the privilege of participation. As each alliance is negotiated someone should inquire if the price is too high.

6

"Maximum Feasible Participation"

The purpose . . . is to provide stimulation and incentive for urban and rural communities to mobilize their resources to combat poverty through community action programs. . . . The term "community action program" means a program—which is developed, conducted and administered with the maximum feasible participation of residents of the areas and members of the groups served. (From Title II of the Economic Opportunity Act of 1964, as amended.)

At a Washington press conference held nearly a year and a half after the first community action program had been funded, poverty war director R. Sargent Shriver was asked, "Please name one specific example of a significant contribution brought about by participation of the poor in a poverty program." After a long pause Shriver replied, "Well, I can think of a lot of philosophical and ideological and emotional evidence. . . . It's very hard for me to think up a concrete example." (Reported in the *Chicago Sun-Times*, February 16, 1966.)

This requirement of "maximum feasible participation" has been the most controversial element in this new war on poverty. Officials of the Office of Economic Opportunity have been criticized by mayors and other local officials because they have pressed too hard for "maximum feasible participation." They also have been criticized by conservative Republicans and by the New Left, by churchmen and by social workers, by civil rights leaders, and by the poor themselves for not insisting on greater participation by the poor.

The most highly visible participation by the churches in the war on poverty has been in community action programs which call for "maximum feasible participation."

The churches have been among the leaders in demanding that the poor be encouraged and permitted to participate in planning and fighting the war. In scores of communities articulate churchmen have worked hard, and sometimes effectively, to insure that the poor would be represented on the board of the local "umbrella" community action committee which supervises and coordinates the distribution of OEO grants for local programs. Literally dozens of resolutions have been officially adopted by religious organizations urging that this section of Title II be meticulously observed.

This provision has moved several religious organizations to seek new and creative methods of involving the poor in the community decision-making process. This phrase has produced some of the most unusual elections ever held in American cities. This provision in the Act has stimulated some of the thinking in the ideological struggle which is

dividing churchmen in the war. This requirement has had
the indirect effect of draining much of the church-supplied
leadership out of the civil rights movement. Each of these
results of this emphasis on "maximum feasible participation"
merits further discussion—but before turning to that it may
be helpful to examine the general implications of this phrase.

First of all, it should be remembered that the poor did not
originate this concept nor was it added by Congress. It was
developed by a handful of middle-class liberal bureaucrats in
Washington, some of whom doubted that it would ever
get out of the Congressional committee. Second, while this is
not an extremely important distinction, it should be pointed
out that the language of the Act does not call literally for
participation of the poor, only for participation by the
"residents of the areas and *members* of the groups served."
Thus the participation could be by people who themselves are
above the poverty line in income, as long as they are residents
of the area or members of the group to be served. In fact,
in the debates before Congressional committees, in staff discussions in OEO, in the Community Action Program Guide
issued by OEO, and in most local communities the wording
has been interpreted to mean "maximum feasible participation
of the poor themselves." [1] This has been the position taken
by those who have sought to gain representation for the poor
on poverty boards. On the other hand, a significant proportion
of the jobs for nonprofessionals in the execution of the pro-

[1] For an excellent analysis of the source and various interpretations of maximum feasible participation, see "Participation of the Poor," *The Yale Law
Journal,* LXXV (March, 1966), 599-629. For a realistic analysis of the
limitations inherent in the concept of participation of the poor, see Earl Raab,
"What War and Which Poverty?" *The Public Interest,* Spring, 1966, pp. 45-56.

grams has been secured by individuals who qualify as "residents" or "members," but who had an income above the poverty level when they went on the anti-poverty payroll.

Four Approaches to Solving the Problem of Poverty

The significance of this idea of maximum feasible participation of the poor can be seen most clearly if the current approaches to the problems of poverty are divided into four categories.

The traditional American approach has been to delegate this responsibility to government and to the organized private philanthropic and charitable organizations. These agencies have been expected to meet the needs of the poor. When this new federally financed war on poverty was launched, the officials of these public and private voluntary agencies assumed that they would be the channels for dispensing these funds at the local level. Tradition and experience were on their side.

When the demand came for maximum feasible participation of the poor, many of these traditional leaders felt threatened. One mayor charged that organizing the poor into politically active groups demanding representation was "undermining the integrity of local government." Another accused Sargent Shriver of "fostering class struggle." [2]

This political interpretation of how the war on poverty should be fought is held by a great many elected public officials. They believe that by virtue of their election to public

[2] Both quotations are from Barbara Carter, "Sargent Shriver and the Role of the Poor," *The Reporter*, May 5, 1966, pp. 17-20.

office they represent all the people including the poor. They tend to regard any attempt to produce greater involvement of the poor through quasi-official bodies as a threat to the orderly processes of government—and to their power.

A second approach to solving local problems such as poverty is to bring the top community leaders together to focus their attention on the issue at hand. Hopefully these leaders will recognize the severity of the problem, develop an appropriate course of action, and use their power to implement this decision. Basically this is an approach from within the community power structure. It is one of the most popular approaches to reform and has many supporters. The Ford Foundation, for example, used this approach in their "Gray Areas" program of the late 1950's. It also has been a favorite of those supporting some form of metropolitan government and of leaders in the voluntary health and welfare agencies.

While this approach has been useful in solving many community problems, it also has failed on many occasions in recent years. Basically it means working with and through the people and agencies firmly committed to the status quo, and therefore it is difficult, if not impossible, to secure changes fast enough to stave off a crisis, much less to solve the more complex problems such as poverty.

A third approach is illustrated by certain forms of militant community organization. The key issues are selected and dramatized, an effort is made to rally the oppressed against the "enemy," and there is no hesitation to resort to conflict to achieve the goal. This approach to effecting social change was used by the labor movement in the 1930's and the civil rights movement in the late 1950's and early 1960's. Basically it is an approach to the problem through the victims of the problem rather than through the so-called community power structure.

The community organization process does help to increase the degree of participation by the poor and it also helps the people gain a greater awareness of their problems. Perhaps even more important, it helps the poor and the oppressed acquire a renewed sense of dignity and worth. Some of the more militant forms of community organization have been especially effective in achieving these two goals. On the other hand the more militant community organizations which emphasize protest as the central organizing theme often are less influential in effecting social change than those organizational efforts that emphasize the project approach such as consumer cooperatives, housing, or community development.

A fourth approach is represented by the idea of maximum feasible participation. Called by some observers "the Wagner Act for the poor," the concept of maximum feasible participation may be a new breakthrough in the American political practice of pluralism.

To some the idea of maximum feasible participation of the poor simply means that the poor must be *represented* in any agency which develops and implements a federally financed anti-poverty program. To others this phrase means the poor must be *involved* in the planning and administration of such a program. The vast difference between *representation* and *involvement* has been one of the major sources of tension and conflict in the administration of the anti-poverty program.

For the first year and a half the Office of Economic Opportunity strongly urged that the poor be involved at the local level. Subsequently, as the political heat rose and as pressures increased to fund and implement action programs, OEO appeared willing to accept either representation or involvement as evidence of participation.

In many communities the great American urge to find a consensus produced an attempt to blend all four of these approaches into one comprehensive effort. Governmental officials, representatives from the private voluntary agencies, and established community leaders usually were willing, often eager, to set up an umbrella agency. Frequently they were joined by representatives from the less militant community organizations which preferred coalitions to conflict, and by those who felt that representation satisfied the requirement for the maximum feasible participation of the poor. In several other communities this attempt to establish an all-inclusive coalition was rejected. The rejection usually came from the leaders of the more militant community organizations who believed that conflict was a useful tool for hastening the pace of social change and from persons who interpreted maximum feasible participation to mean involvement.

The churches and churchmen have been active in all four of these approaches to the problem of poverty. Active and dedicated churchmen can be found in the legislative and administrative branches of government, in the private voluntary social welfare agencies, and in nearly all forms of community organization. The churches have long been active in attempting to contact and influence all three of these structures of society. In recent months, however, the most creative efforts of the churches have been directed toward achieving the goal of the maximum feasible participation of the poor. Five different methods of involving the poor in the war on poverty have attracted the interest of the churches and therefore merit closer attention.

Maximizing the Participation of the Poor

The least controversial of the various efforts to involve the poor has been the move to hire indigenous leadership as nonprofessional workers in various anti-poverty programs. The poor have been hired to survey the neighborhood, to help organize the community, to assist professional teachers in child development classes, to conduct neighborhood recreational programs, and for similar ventures.[3] Many churches have participated in this indirectly through federally financed anti-poverty programs, and a few have added indigenous leadership to the paid staff of the church. This move to employ the indigenous poor for program implementation has been one of the least publicized, but one of the most important, breakthroughs in this new war on poverty. When the poor are employed to implement the program designed to help the poor, a type of involvement is possible that has many benefits, some of which can be achieved in no other way. This approach stands in sharp contrast to earlier programs which were geared to serve the poor, but which usually were developed, planned, and implemented by "outsiders" without involving the poor.

[3] For a provocative presentation of this dimension of the involvement of the poor, see Arthur Pearl and Frank Riessman, *New Careers for the Poor* (New York: The Free Press, 1965).

Unquestionably the most controversial effort by the churches to maximize the participation of the poor has grown out of an earlier approach to the problem of poverty and emphasized the community organization process as a means of acquiring power. The most widely known exponent of this concept is Saul D. Alinsky and his organization, the Industrial Areas Foundation (IAF). Alinsky and community organizers with a similar philosophy have been called in by church groups in a score of cities to help organize the poor and gain for them a voice at the bargaining table where community decisions are made. [4] The United Presbyterian Church in the U. S. A. and the Episcopal Church have been the two Protestant denominations that have provided the greatest degree of support for this approach. Both these denominations have supported the efforts of local churches to use Alinsky's methodology in organizing the poor. Two of the best known products of this approach are TWO in Chicago and FIGHT in Rochester, New York.

A third approach to involve the poor in the anti-poverty effort was based on the idea that participation can be achieved by enabling the poor to elect their own representatives to serve on the local anti-poverty board which administered the community action program. This appeared to be a democratic means of achieving the goal of maximum feasible participation, and in several cities this idea of participation through elections was energetically supported by the churches.

[4] For two different interpretations of this form of community organization, see Lyle E. Schaller, *Community Organization: Conflict and Reconciliation* (Nashville: Abingdon Press, 1966), pp. 90-114, and Charles E. Silberman, *Crisis in Black and White* (New York: Random House, 1964), pp. 317-58.

The results were disappointing. In the first year and a half of the war elections were held in seven cities—Boston; Chester, Pa.; Cleveland; Huntsville, Ala.; Kansas City, Mo.; Los Angeles; and Philadelphia. The combined result was that over ninety-seven percent of those eligible to vote did not do so. The two best responses were in Huntsville where sixteen percent of the eligible voters cast ballots and in Chester where six percent voted. In Los Angeles only 0.7 percent of the 400,000 eligibles voted. Later an election in Denver produced ten percent turnout while a second election in Philadelphia in July 1966 found 7.7 percent of the 350,000 eligible persons casting votes.

The low turnout disappointed those churchmen who had devoted large quantities of time and energy to this venture. Later they explained that perhaps they had failed to perceive that an election is really a middle-class institution and might not appeal to the poor. Other reasons were offered for the low level of participation—the reluctance of some to identify themselves as poor, the dependence on middle-class communication media to reach the poor with the result that many poor people did not even know an election was to be held, the feeling in several cities that, since the representatives to be elected would constitute only a minority on the board, the election was unimportant, and the lack of resources necessary to stage a good campaign and thus arouse interest among the apathetic electorate.

Some churchmen, however, were even more disappointed by other aspects of the elections. A few argued that the $127,000 spent on these elections (over 3 dollars per vote)

103

could have been spent more creatively on other anti-poverty efforts. Others who had hoped that the elections would increase the interest of adult males in the anti-poverty program and thus break down the matriarchal pattern of life in the ghetto were disappointed. In Cleveland, for example, forty of the forty-eight candidates and four of the five winners were women.

Perhaps the most disappointing result of this attempt to increase the participation through elections was that the people elected soon ceased to be recognized by the poor as their spokesmen. Those who hoped the elections would produce leaders who could truly represent the poor were disillusioned when among the winners were candidates with a close identification with a political organization or the colonial empire of a voluntary welfare agency. A recurring theme when the House Committee on Education and Labor held hearings on an extension and expansion of the anti-poverty program was that, whenever a representative of the poor was placed on a local community action board, he soon was being accused of no longer representing the poor. While some of these charges may be baseless, there is an inherent danger in depending upon representation as an adequate means of involving the poor in this or any other program.

This dissatisfaction with the alternative of achieving involvement and a meaningful voice for the poor through elected representation has produced a variety of suggestions. Some people contend that the only way to gain meaningful participation for the poor is to turn the anti-poverty funds over to the poor and let them spend the money. Most public officials recoil in horror from such suggestions, perhaps because they regard this as an irresponsible delegation of their authority, perhaps because they recognize that the authority to allocate the expenditure of public funds is a source of power, and they are reluctant to surrender that power.

One of the most creative alternatives to come from the churches has been the idea of creating an organization and then turning it over to the poor for them to run. This is based on the assumption that a person, regardless of income, has a right to make choices in a democratic society. In the neighborhoods where the poor live, however, they have far fewer choices. Those on relief do not choose their own case worker. The sick often are not able to choose their own doctor or hospital. The Negro has only a limited choice in his place of residence. The poor seldom have an effective choice in the location or operation of the public schools in their neighborhoods, or in the planning or implementation of urban renewal programs that may change the face of their neighborhood.

To have these choices, people must have power, and one means of gaining this power is to have their own "government."

In Columbus, Ohio, First English Lutheran Church has undertaken to provide the poor in its neighborhood with their own "government." Once a middle- and upper-class congregation, in the late 1950's this congregation developed a social settlement type program to serve the Negroes and rural whites moving into the neighborhood. When the shortcomings of this approach became apparent the pastor, the Rev. Leopold W. Bernhard, sought a new approach. After consultation with Dr. Milton Kotler of the Institute for Policy Studies, it was decided to establish a neighborhood foundation which would be a "self-governing, tax-exempt corporation for total community service." The goal was to create a base for public decision-making at the ward or neighborhood level of the city and "to further the welfare of the community by self-determined program development and management." The governing of an existing church settlement house would be turned over to the people it was created to serve. An OEO grant of $26,000 was secured to finance the first three months of the life of this new direct membership community organization called the East Central Citizens Organization (ECCO). During these months an interim committee arranged for the adoption of by-laws, election of the first regular Executive Council from among the residents of the area, and preparation of preliminary program plans. On March 1, 1966, the entire organization was "turned over" to indigenous leadership, and the formal ties with the church were severed. A $158,000 OEO grant provided the operational funds for the first year.[5]

This is truly a pioneering venture. The church created and launched the organization, but once launched it is *completely* independent of the church. All decisions on policy and program in ECCO are made by the residents. Any resident eighteen and over can become a member of the Assembly. The Assembly elects an executive council, and each member

[5] For two contrasting accounts of the origins and goals of ECCO, see James Ridgeway, "Missionaries in Darkest Ohio," *The New Republic*, February 5, 1966, pp. 9-10, and Abe Z. Zaidan, "We Were Sunday Invaders," *The Lutheran*, June 22, 1966, pp. 6-10.

of the council receives $1,000 per year for his expenses, and this helps to insure that he will take his job seriously. All programs must be approved by the Assembly. Outside professionals may be hired to carry out the program, but the structure is designed to make sure that the professionals do not become the bosses. ECCO stands in sharp contrast to the traditional efforts at meeting the needs of the poor in a specific geographical area. In the most common type of organization the nonresidents who provide the funds and the nonresident professional staff develop and implement the program. More recently, especially under OEO grants, an effort has been made to include a few of the indigenous poor on the policy-making board and on the staff. In ECCO the *entire* responsibility for program development is vested in indigenous leadership.

While it is too early to evaluate the success of this program, ECCO stands as one of the most creative experiments by the churches to achieve maximum participation by the poor. Will the programs developed by a self-governing neighborhood agency be different from those developed by the more traditional type of organization? Will the poor be more liberal or more conservative in their attitude toward change?

While ECCO is notable as an attempt to maximize the participation of the residents of a depressed neighborhood in the administration of a neighborhood organization, the fact remains that the idea and the establishment of the original structure was largely the creation of outsiders. In Cleveland a different approach has been attempted. There several denominations created the Protestant Ministry to Poverty with the Rev. Paul Younger as director. After several months in this post Younger became convinced that the central need was to enable the poor to organize themselves independently and outside the structure of a "managed" welfare society. Instead of turning to the churches or to outside organizers for help in creating such an organization, Younger turned to the poor themselves. Out of this came the proposal known as EHOFA (Eastern Hough Organized for Action).

An application for a demonstration grant was made to OEO so that EHOFA could "employ neighborhood residents to develop organizations or residents . . . (who) together will carry out activities and actions to combat the conditions of poverty in their area, producing changes in themselves, their immediate environment, and the major service systems involved in the area."

Two of the central emphases of the EHOFA approach are (1) the value of self-help and (2) the need to increase the capacity of the poor to act on their own behalf. In order to participate effectively they need confidence, knowledge, and skills. EHOFA provides the frame work which enables the poor to acquire confidence, knowledge, and skills through a self-help type of procedure. To insure that this will happen, the EHOFA proposal places the decision-making power for development and the use of community resources and services in the hands of the poor themselves and reduces the professional to a consultant role.

EHOFA differs from ECCO in that in Cleveland the emphasis was in involving indigenous leadership from the very beginning and enabling them to create their own organization. EHOFA encountered grave difficulties in securing an OEO grant, and it is questionable whether sufficient funds can be secured locally to finance the effort. On the other hand it is possible that local financing would enhance the effectiveness of such an indigenous organization.

While these five different categories of efforts to maximize the participation of the poor do not include all the efforts by the churches, they do illustrate several approaches developed to achieve that goal. More time and experience are needed before these different approaches can receive an adequate evaluation.

The Ideological Struggle

This emphasis on involvement of the poor also has contributed to an ideological debate that has produced a sharp division among churchmen. The origins of this current debate go back beyond the beginning of the new poverty war to the civil rights movement.

While oversimplifications sometimes confuse as much as they clarify, it may be helpful in describing the current ideological struggle to break the political spectrum into four segments. At one extreme is the radical right. Members of this group are dissatisfied with *both* the system or structures that constitute American life *and* with the way the system works. They believe a major change in the system is required before their goals can be achieved. The most distinctive characteristic of members of this group is their dislike of a large and powerful federal government. In many respects they would like to reverse the results of the Civil War and of the New Deal. The John Birch Society is at this end of the spectrum as are many of the militant segregationists in the nation.

To the immediate left of that group are those who might be labeled conservatives. They have come to accept the system but have a few reservations about how it is working. They have accepted the idea of "Big Government" and have become accustomed to seeing a magazine such as *Fortune* support many of the policies and actions of the federal government. The eastern liberal wing of the Republican Party can be found in this political grouping. In general, those who find this a comfortable spot on the political spectrum are not opposed to change, but they are opposed to rapid social changes and to changes which they do not influence or guide.

The third category is further to the left along the political spectrum and includes those who are satisfied with the system in general, but dissatisfied with the way it works. They could be called the "old" liberals and include those who support a larger role for the federal government in the economy, in the war on poverty, in the solution of metropolitan problems, and in the civil rights struggle. Members of this group tend to believe that more aggressive action by the federal government will open up opportunities for the Negro, the poor, and the oppressed, to rise to new achievements within the present basic structures of society. Many of the members of this segment of the political spectrum trace their formative years back to the Great Depression, the New Deal, and the Fair Deal.

On the extreme left is the fourth and probably smallest group. The members of this group are sometimes labeled

"The New Left," often identify themselves as "radicals," and perhaps can best be described as the "new liberals." They are dissatisfied with *both* the system *and* the way it is working.[6] In civil rights they point out that despite all the successes and all the federal activity every index shows that segregation by race is increasing. They insist that increasing the power of the federal government benefits the middle and upper classes, not the poor. They point to the military draft to illustrate their contention that the system is basically wrong. The draft now bears most heavily on the poor, the student from an inadequate slum school, the teen-ager who cannot go to college, and the underprivileged. In analyzing the war on poverty these new liberals contend that it is really a war on the poor, on the value system of the poor and on their culture. The war is not really directed toward the causes of poverty, they argue, and they contend that most of the dollars expended so far have found their way into the pockets of the middle-class professionals who have been living off the poor for years. The radicals believe that the liberals in their efforts to open up and improve the functioning of the system completely ignore the only realistic approach which is to junk the present system of social

[6] For two very perceptive and provocative analyses of the radical new left from a liberal perspective, see Michael Harrington, "The Mystical Militants," *The New Republic,* February 10, 1966, pp. 20-22, and Paul Seabury, "Gideon's Army and Moynihan's Pros," *The New Republic,* March 19, 1966, pp. 23-25. For two other very penetrating analyses of this growing split between those who believe reform can be accomplished within the existing structures of society and those who contend this is impossible, see Sidney Lens, "The New Left—and the Old," *The Progressive,* June, 1966, pp. 19-24, and Steven Kelman, "The Feud Among the Radicals," *Harper's Magazine,* June, 1966, pp. 67-79.

structures as inherently evil and substitute for it a new and more egalitarian system of relationships and distribution of power. Members of this end of the political spectrum tend to be younger than those in the liberal or conservative groups, and many reached adulthood during or after the Eisenhower era. The roots of this group are in the civil rights movement and in the war on poverty. Only later did international relations arouse the interest of the new left.

The clearest illustration of this division between the old liberal and the new left can be seen in the civil rights movement. On the one hand there are civil rights leaders and groups who believe that the goal of a desegregated society can be achieved within the framework of existing social, economic, and political structures. This liberal group includes individuals such as Martin Luther King, Roy Wilkins, and Bayard Rustin, and organizations such as the Urban League, the National Association for the Advancement of Colored People (NAACP), and the Southern Christian Leadership Conference (SCLC). Those adhering to this position contend that reform can be achieved by altering the distribution of power within the existing structures of society. A contrasting and more radical position is represented by organizations such as the Student Non-Violent Coordinating Committee (SNCC), Students for a Democratic Society (SDS), and the Mississippi Freedom Democratic Party (MFDP). Most of the leaders of these organizations argue that it is immoral to seek and unrealistic to expect reforms by working through the established structures. They insist that the goals of desegregation and social justice can be achieved only by setting up new structures, even if this means destroying the old organizations which have provided a base of operation for the liberal.

While the civil rights movement was the first place in which this split between the liberals and the radicals became highly visible, it soon spread to many other segments of society. In June of 1966, a member of the new left opposed an incumbent liberal congressman in the Democratic primary in California and, while he was defeated, he did receive 45 percent of the votes cast. One of the leading radical supporters of the loser stated very clearly that this was not an attempt to "take over" the Democratic Party but rather was designed to destroy it. Similar conflicts between the liberals and the radicals can be found in other parts of the Democratic Party (a close parallel is the efforts of the Radical Right to destroy the Republican Party), in the social work profession, and in the churches.

This growing division between the old liberals and the new liberals or radicals has been ignored by many conservative and liberal churchmen who fail to understand the perspective of the New Left. The old liberal churchman thinks that he and his colleagues on the immediate left are allies in one great war and that the petty differences in political philosophy can be ignored.

The new radical looks around to see who is supporting the system which he feels must be changed before progress can be achieved and sees as his immediate opponent the old liberal who appears to articulate the same desire for social justice, but apparently fails to see that the functioning

113

of the system makes the achievement of social justice an impossibility. The natural reaction of the radical is that the old liberal is part of the "enemy" and must be attacked. The natural response of the old liberal is, "Why are you attacking me; I am the best friend and ally you have. It's those over there (pointing to the conservatives and the radical right) who are the real enemy!"

The radical argues, "As long as you support the basic system of our society, you are perpetuating structures which automatically keep the poor and the oppressed from getting a fair deal. In order to end racial segregation and to eradicate poverty, we must revolutionize society. Simple reform is not enough!"

The debate continues. The liberal contends that he is a liberal by conviction, that he believes in the basic structures of society, that government is a legitimate order of creation, and that while the sinful nature of man means it is impossible to completely reform society, much has been accomplished and more is possible without resorting to an overthrow of the existing structures of society.

The radical responds that increasing the size of the highway appropriation may produce bigger and safer roads, but that "sprinkling on more welfare money" will not solve the poverty problem. He challenges the liberal by asking, "Are you a liberal by conviction, or only because your life is so completely entrenched in the middle-class power structure of our society that you feel threatened if someone suggests that the structure is evil and must be changed if progress is to be achieved?"

Participatory Democracy

While it is not the central issue in the war on poverty, one of the most important concepts to emerge out of this effort to maximize the participation of the poor is "participatory democracy." Participatory democracy is one of the favorite themes of the new left. It is unquestionably the most optimistic doctrine offered as a method of solving the problems of the poor. It is either the most promising or the most illusory proposal for improving democratic procedures in America. It is also the type of proposal which is helpful in distinguishing the viewpoint of the new left from that of the old liberals.

Basically this phrase is a plea for increasing the degree of participation by the people in the democratic process. Thus this concept forms the basis for the demand that the people who live in the neighborhood, not the planners and officials in city hall, should determine the nature of any urban renewal program that threatens to uproot the residents, destroy their homes, wipe out the small businesses, and break up lifelong friendship patterns and interpersonal relationships. This concept is behind the plea that the recipients of public assistance should have a voice in the development and administration of the welfare programs that provide them with a livelihood. Many community organization efforts, such as TWO in Chicago, FIGHT in Rochester, ECCO in Columbus, and EHOFA in Cleveland, have been based in large part on this idea of participatory democracy.

Some liberals, when they see the enthusiasm displayed by both radicals and other liberals for this concept, brush it

115

off rather lightly as far from a new idea in American history. The long list of American proponents of participatory democracy would include Jefferson, Thoreau, William Jennings Bryan, and Barry Goldwater. This list would also include the Populists; the writers of many state constitutions; the turn-of-the-century advocates of the recall, the referendum, and the initiative; the proponents of "states' rights," and the opponents of fair housing legislation.

The current definition of the phrase "participatory democracy" is a far more revolutionary concept than any of the earlier efforts to broaden the base of *continuing* participation in the decision-making process.

Historically most Americans have agreed with Woodrow Wilson that our system called for popular control over government but not popular participation in the day-to-day processes of decision-making. There are a few major exceptions to this, such as the initiative, the referendum, and the mandatory public hearing, but basically ours is a system of representative democracy.[7]

The anti-poverty program is the first formal governmental effort to directly involve the poor in the planning and administration of a program intended to help those in need. It has tremendous potential for broadening the base of the political system and for the advancement of democracy. If maximum feasible participation does spark a move toward participatory democracy, it probably will be the major contribution of the entire anti-poverty program.

[7] An excellent analysis of the potential of participatory democracy is found in Peter Marcuse, "The Anti-Poverty Program," *Pratt Planning Papers*, III (October, 1965), 21-36.

The whole concept of participatory democracy, however, is vulnerable to being oversold. While it could enhance and enlarge the democratic process, it alone will not end poverty or correct all the other ills of society.

First of all, it may not be the best method of accelerating the pace of social change—and that appears to be a major goal of many advocates of participatory democracy. Past experiences with the concept often have produced conservative reactions from the people. Participatory democracy can be found in many states and cities where a referendum is required before the tax rate can be raised. In general these communities have a lower level of public services than are found in cities where the elected representatives can increase the tax rate without a referendum. The fragmentation of local government in nearly all the nation's metropolitan areas is a direct result of the desire for participatory democracy. The defeat of several fair housing laws and ordinances occurred only because participatory democracy made a referendum possible. In Protestant church circles the Baptists are the strongest proponents of participatory democracy, and the result has produced a denominational structure with very limited effectiveness. The historical record seems to suggest to many liberals that participatory democracy and rapid social change are incompatible goals.

This suggests that the new wave of interest in participatory democracy may not produce great social gains unless it also can produce new forms of participation. This may be the key. It may be true that not all cultural groups make decisions in the same way and that new structures must be discovered

117

to enable the poor to have an effective and meaningful voice in the decision-making process. A few of the more innovative anti-poverty programs have attempted to develop interesting new structures for community decision-making such as the community convention, the neighborhood "town meeting," and various highly informal meetings.

Perhaps more important than the *process* of decision-making is the *implementation* of decisions. Thus far the advocates of participatory democracy have emphasized the need to involve more people in the decision-making process and have neglected the subject of how these decisions will be implemented. They have stressed the value of protest and the acquisition of the veto power. Little has been said or done about enabling the poor to acquire the skills necessary for administration. As one critic of this romanticized concept of participatory democracy points out, "It is administration which can implement the hopes of a protest group, implement them precisely through the complex routines of bureaucracy." [8] Unless the participatory democrats are able to send large numbers of their own people into the bureaucracy of government, it is doubtful that they can make many positive contributions affecting the pace and direction of social change. It often is easier to acquire political power than it is to convert that power into progressive action programs.

There is also the danger that participatory democracy has been oversold as *the* solution to all the problems, rather than

[8] Karl Hertz, "A Utopian Tract," *The Lutheran Quarterly,* XVIII (February, 1966), 26. For another statement of this fundamental point, see Edgar S. Cahn and Jean C. Cahn, "The War on Poverty: A Civilian Perspective," *The Yale Law Journal,* LXXIII (July, 1964), 1333.

as a part of the solution to a part of a very complex problem. As one middle-aged liberal who has been an ardent supporter of the need for maximum feasible participation said,

Let's not expect miracles from this idea of the participation of the poor lest we make the helpless responsible for their own condition. Can we expect all of the poor to break out of poverty simply by giving them leadership opportunities? Will this solve the problems of the husbandless woman with seven kids? The aged? The illiterate? Will it solve the problems of my brother in poverty who is old, colored, sick, ignorant and whipped and whose soul has been crushed from the day he was born? Let's not delude ourselves with romantic and simple solution to problems that are a product of a very complex set of causes!

Tensions Produced by This Ideological Conflict

The differences in viewpoint between the liberal and the radical have already affected the churches' participation in the war on poverty. They have produced several areas of tension which have been very divisive. These ideological differences and the resulting tensions probably will prevent a completely unified approach by the churches to the problems of poverty. The divisive effect of these emotion-laden differences of opinion can be seen by a brief examination of several of the outstanding points of conflict.

1. *Coalitions or Conflict?*

What is the best strategy for winning the war on poverty? The answer to this question is greatly influenced by the respondent's frame of reference. The liberal and the pragmatist urge the formation of alliances and coalitions, while the radical and the idealist tend to resist any move toward cooperation and often find themselves in conflict with potential allies. [9] The ideological split described earlier suggests that it will be impossible for American churchmen to agree on a common strategy.

2. The Role of Government

Much of the criticism of the government's anti-poverty programs has been based on the assumption that governmental actions should be directed by ideological motivations. The demands on government by those at the left end of the political spectrum reflect this point of view. Those at the other end of the political alignment, the radical right, also operate from this premise. Both believe the government should be "for" certain ideals and "against" other values.

Whether government *should* be motivated primarily by ideological considerations is not the point here, however. The fact is that in America government has two basic roles, (1) to provide services, and (2) to resolve conflicts among conflicting groups and subgroups in the social system. In this nation, government is not primarily ideologically oriented. While many people in government do hold and express a clearly defined ideological position, the institutional pressures usually reduce this to the level of a secondary consideration in the decision-making process.

This fact of life is accepted by most conservatives and old-line liberals as they work with governmental programs

[9] An excellent brief on behalf of the coalition approach is John David Maguire, "Will We Lose the War on Poverty?" *Christianity and Crisis,* April 18, 1966, pp. 71-74. Maguire calls for an alliance of the poor, the professors, the politicians, and the administrators, contending that any one group can wreck the program by failing to cooperate.

in the war on poverty. It is rejected by many of the people on the new left. The result is more than a difference of opinion over the role of government. It is a source of conflict over goals, priorities, strategies, and tactics.

3. *Practical Politics Versus Idealism*

A closely related source of tension is that many idealistic churchmen expect that they can enter the political arena, work for their goals, and avoid the compromises and struggles for power which characterize the political scene.

Experience clearly demonstrates that the political forces of the community are attracted to all facets of social change. This can be seen in the civil rights movement, in urban renewal, and in the war on poverty. When the political pressures begin to be felt, there comes a choosing of sides. The radical idealist is repelled by this and appalled by the way some of his liberal pragmatic associates are able to adjust and continue to function.

This conflict between idealism and the realities of the political scene already has divided well-intentioned churchmen and church groups who feel constrained to share in the national effort to eliminate poverty.

While many of the old liberals are able to accept and adjust to the inevitable compromises, the people on the new left often conclude that the only way they can maintain their integrity is to function from outside the system, attack it, and do everything they can to create a crisis which cannot be resolved by compromise, and thus cause the system to break down.

4. *The Community Decision-Making Process*

Just as members of the new left mistakenly expect the

government to act from ideological motivations, they also believe that decision makers in other nongovernmental segments of the community should be ready and willing to stand up and be counted, as community issues are defined in black and white terms. Whether community leaders *should* behave this way is not the issue here. The important point is that in real life the community decision-making process is basically a nonideological operation. It is a very pragmatic problem-solving operation and functions in the ways necessary to relieve tensions, to minimize open conflict, and to achieve a compromise acceptable to all parties.

In general, old liberals find it much easier to function in this process than do members of the new left. The result is that the radicals accuse the liberals of being too willing to "do business with the enemy," while the liberals conclude that the radicals are simply being unrealistic about life.

5. *Financing the Revolution*

One of the unique characteristics of this revolutionary concept that calls for the maximum feasible participation of the poor, the replacement of the old structures of society, and the establishment of a new philosophical base for the allocation of national resources centers on the question of financing. The demand is that those against whom the revolution is directed should finance the cost. While it is true that nearly all revolutions in history have been financed by middle classes, that is not an adequate parallel for this demand. Today the holders of power are being asked to provide the funds for the programs which are intended to reduce their power. The most highly visible example of this is the pressure placed on mayors to approve community action projects which are designed to attack the structures and powers of local government and of the political leaders in office.

This issue of how the revolution is to be financed is already beginning to produce tensions and conflicts in both the public and the private agencies involved in the war on poverty. Perhaps this can best be illustrated by looking at the churches. The ecclesiastical bureaucrats responsible for general supervision in the denominational headquarters, as in government, tend to be middle-aged liberals and conservatives with a strong pragmatic streak in their make-up. Most of the radical clergymen are young, eager, idealistic, iconoclastic ministers out in the field "where the action is." If they fail, little will be heard; if they succeed, fireworks are inevitable.

"Right now one half of my salary is paid by my denomination and one half by a grant from OEO," said one of these self-styled young radicals. "If I am successful in my efforts to organize the poor here and help them gain a meaningful voice in the decisions that affect their lives, both the denomination and OEO will feel a tremendous amount of pressure to cut off the funds for this project. My only question is whether my Bishop will cut off his support before Sargent Shriver terminates his grant."[10]

6. *Social Justice or Love and Reconciliation?*

Within the Christian community the greatest difference of opinion growing out of this ideological split concerns purposes, goals, and methods. One group contends that the

---

[10] A parallel to this in ecclesiastical circles is found in the efforts of several groups who are out to eliminate denominationalism in American Protestantism and who seek the funds for these efforts from denominational treasuries.

123

primary responsibility of the individual Christian and of the church is reconciliation. They believe that the Christian, acting from a motive of love, must always seek to be a reconciling force in a society divided along racial, economic, and social lines.

Another group of equally committed Christians insists that the highest goal a loving Christian can seek in a sinful world is social justice.

Each side has a tendency to rationalize its methods on the basis of its goals. Each group has a difficult time understanding the ethical basis of the other's position. Each group has an even more difficult time understanding the actions of the other.

How seriously these and similar divisions will affect the churches' involvement in the war on poverty remains to be seen. It is also too early to tell how these ideological differences will influence the outcome of the war. It does appear, however, that because of the nature of the processes at work, the new left is doomed to lose most of the battles but may win the war. This is the nature of many ideological revolutions. The existing structures of society will accommodate themselves to the ideas and goals of the new left and accept many of their proposals and programs. Thus as labor gained a seat at the bargaining table in the 1930's, the poor are acquiring their place in the 1960's. The concept of welfare benefits is being converted into an acceptance of the right of every citizen to have adequate shelter, food, and clothing. The privilege of a college education is becoming a right.

Group conflict is being accepted as having useful functions in a well-integrated pluralistic society.

By 1997, the members of the new left of the mid-1960's may find themselves under attack for their conservative and pragmatic attitudes.

The Diversion of Civil Rights Leadership

An unforeseen result of the emphasis on the maximum participation of indigenous leadership in the anti-poverty effort has been the depletion of the leadership in the civil rights movement. This is somewhat ironic, for many of the churchmen who were the strongest supporters of the struggle for racial equality have discovered that their demands for involvement of the poor in the war on poverty have weakened the civil rights movement. The time and energy of key leaders in the civil rights movement has been diverted to anti-poverty programs.

The allegation is frequently heard that indigenous civil rights leaders have been "bought off" with jobs financed out of OEO grants. While it may be possible to cite a few examples to support this thesis, the allegation is untrue and unfair. The issues of race and poverty are so closely interwoven that it is easy to understand how a person who had devoted much or all of his time to the civil rights movement could accept a full-time position in an anti-poverty program and believe that this would enable him to be a greater influence in improving the lot of the impoverished Negro. An important, but as yet unanswered question is whether this was a wise move. As an increasing number of community action programs began to experience difficulty in being funded, some former civil rights leaders began to wonder if they had made the right move.

While it is easy to understand why many active civil rights leaders gravitated to staff positions in anti-poverty programs, it also must be recognized that while the issues of race and poverty are interrelated and do overlap, they are not simply two sides of the same coin. In many respects they are different and much of the energy spent in the war on poverty has had absolutely no impact on the problem of racial discrimination.

The effects of this diversion can be seen by looking at the civil rights movement, especially in northern cities, and observing the decreased level of interest, activity, and support.

The effects of this diversion can be seen even more clearly in the churches. The churchmen, both lay and clerical, who yesterday were marching on the picket lines, sitting-in at restaurants, and attending mass rallies, are no longer there. Today they are running Head Start programs or developing work schedules for the Neighborhood Youth Corps. Today they are working their way through snarls of red tape and piles of official documents preparing requests for anti-poverty grants. Today, instead of attacking the strongholds of discrimination, they are attacking the local community anti-poverty boards to increase the representation of the poor on these boards or to gain approval for their program proposals. Today, instead of talking glibly about CORE, NAACP, SCLC, and SNCC, they are concerned with a different set of acronyms—OEO, CAP, NYC, and VISTA.

Does the Church Speak for the Poor?

This goal of maximizing the participation of the poor in the war on poverty has produced unforeseen tensions and raised many questions.

One that has been seriously neglected is the extent to which the churches have actually involved the poor in planning church-sponsored anti-poverty programs. There appears to be considerable evidence to support the contention that churchmen have assumed that public officials cannot speak for the poor, but that clergymen, churches, and councils of churches can. If the churches and religious agencies that are sponsoring anti-poverty programs had had a better record on reaching and involving the poor in the past, there would be less basis for raising this question. During the first years of this new war it appeared, however, that too many church-sponsored anti-poverty programs were planned by the churches *for* the poor rather than *with* the poor.

This is not as strange as it may first appear, for the larger Protestant denominations certainly have not been very successful in involving the poor in decision-making within the churches. This is true at both the local church and the denominational levels of church administration. Most denominational conventions and conferences are based on the principle of representative government rather than participatory democracy, and the time and place is usually set in a manner that excludes the poor—with the possible exception of a few low-income retired individuals. Natural institutional pressures in the local church tend to relegate the poor to the sidelines and to lift the individual with salable middle-class skills into leadership positions.

There is an ever-present danger that middle-class church-men who have sought to identify themselves with the poor will conclude that this involvement enables them to speak, not only on behalf of the poor, but also as the voice of the poor. There is a difference.

Perhaps the real call to the churches is not to try to speak for the poor, but rather to fight to keep the door open so that the poor may speak for themselves. As the federally financed war on poverty becomes increasingly institutional-ized, as this effort is gradually "taken over" by the existing middle-class-oriented structures of society, and as the original "indigenous spokesmen for the poor" move up the economic ladder and out of the poverty class, it will become even more difficult to achieve maximum feasible participation of the poor.[11] As this happens, the critical and prophetic voices of the church will be needed more than ever if this original goal of the Economic Opportunity Act is to be achieved.

[11] There is a real question whether these indigenous spokesmen *ever* are truly representative of the poor. Professors Don R. Bowen and Louis H. Masotti of Western Reserve University conducted extensive interviews with forty-three of the forty-eight candidates who sought election to the Cleveland poverty board in early 1966. While the median annual income of the candidates was under $2,500, the candidates tended personally not to identify themselves with the "poor." The researchers also found the candidates to be "one of the most non-alienated group of people who exist."

7

Neglected Issues

During the early months and years of this new war on poverty the emphasis has been largely on action, on launching exciting attacks on the enemy, and on getting new programs started. The churches have shared in this action-oriented response to the call. Comparatively little time or energy has been directed to a consideration of many of the issues which should be high on the churches' agendas. What are the issues which merit the attention of the churches? Have some questions been neglected in the rush to mobilize?

Mission—Or Substitute for Mission?

Perhaps the most seriously neglected issue revolves around the question of the churches' mission. What is the purpose of the church? Does that statement of purpose give direction to the churchmen who are seeking to discover their church's role in this war?

Thus far most of the Protestant churches in America have avoided any direct participation in this new war on poverty. A relatively few churches and church agencies have plunged into battle in a very active manner. Why this variation in response? Is it because of a difference in definition of mission? In leadership? In resources? In location? A comparison of the churches that are actively involved with those which have assumed a more passive role suggests that the difference is not a result of location or resources.

Why does a local church, a larger parish, or a council of churches alter its program plans, readjust its priorities, and change its budget allocations to share in a Head Start program or participate in a new ministry to migrants? Does this represent a change in definition of mission? Is this a move to give the action-oriented members an outlet for their activist spirit? Or can this be explained as simply the normal response to a new opportunity for service and ministry?

Obviously there is no single, simple, and universal explanation. There is, however, a basis for asking whether this sudden burst of interest by some churches is a response to mission or whether it is a substitute for mission. Is participation an expression of relevance or only an appearance of relevance?

In one church it appears that the pastor and a few laymen had been trying for years to get the congregation to feel a sense of mission to the world. Just when they were ready to give this up as a losing battle, the poverty program came along. It provided an easy and low-cost (in dollars) opportunity for this local church to participate in what promised to be a significant social-welfare effort. The church could be in mission! The pastor became involved in the planning and execution of the program. He found what appeared to be a productive outlet for his energies and his desire to make his church relevant to the needs of the people in the neighborhood. The handful of concerned lay leaders saw this as an opportunity to justify the existence of the church in the neighborhood.

The rest of the members—or at least those who were aware of what was happening—were pleased. Their pastor was busy and appeared to be getting what he wanted. It was not going to affect the budget, all their church had to do was to provide space for the program, and janitorial service. They could share in the churches' war on poverty without being involved. In addition their young minister just might become so involved in this that he would stop harassing them about integration and the race question. Perhaps he might even stop talking about "being in mission" and begin preaching the Bible again.

Is this mission—or a substitute for mission?

The same question can be raised about the participation of councils of churches, larger parishes, denominational agencies, and similar groups. Is their involvement in the war on poverty consistent with their mission? Or are they revising their statement of purpose to accommodate this new involvement? Is this what they should be doing—or a substitute for what they should be doing?

Questions such as these are raised to suggest that involvement in the war on poverty should be a product of purpose or mission, not a glamorous and exciting substitute for mission.

The Churches as a Third Force?

One of the most intriguing suggestions, but one which has received comparatively little attention, is that the churches may have a unique role as a "third party," standing between the poor and those community agencies which are organized to serve the poor. This has been proposed as a role for the community action agency,[1] but it also suggests some interesting possibilities for the churches. This role would enable the churches to be free to speak to both the poor and to those who control the policies and resources of the anti-poverty program, it would permit the churches a greater degree of freedom in the allocation of their own resources than they have when they ally themselves with the federal government, it would provide opportunities for new and creative efforts, and it would give the churches greater leverage by enabling them to determine when and where they want to intervene in the war.[2] Two illustrations of how churches have translated this idea into programs are church-sponsored legal-aid clinics and sponsorship of consumer cooperatives.

This is not intended to suggest that *all* churches should seek to become a third party in this national effort, but it does stand out as an option which should not be totally neglected. It offers the opportunity for creative involvement without the restrictions of an alliance.

[1] Martin Rein and Frank Riessman, "A Strategy for Anti-Poverty Community Action Programs," *Social Work*, April, 1966, pp. 3-12.

[2] For a provocative analysis of significant intervention points in the war on poverty, see Joseph Bensman and Emanuel Tobier, "Anti-Poverty Programming: A Proposal," *Urban Affairs Quarterly*, September, 1965, pp. 62-65.

Grantsmanship and Finances

One of the most attractive features of this new war is the generous financial assistance offered to allies by the federal government. An ally with an acceptable plan can obtain a grant from the Office of Economic Opportunity covering ninety percent of the cost of implementation. This is a real challenge to the grantsmanship skill of many a church bureaucrat. He can "do good," build his empire, and impress his board members all at once. In addition, since the local ten percent can be supplied by contributions of staff time, equipment, and building space, it may not really cost his church or agency anything in direct cash outlay.

Often overlooked in this process are three fundamental questions that do merit scrutiny.

First of all, is this new program consistent with the allocation of resources that had been spelled out in the budget? Or does this really mean that the allocations of resources are being amended in order to obtain some "easy" money? Who determines how resources are to be allocated? The Board? Or anyone who comes along with an attractive and heavily subsidized program?

Second, the Economic Opportunity Act of 1964 set a clear limitation on federal assistance for community action programs. During the first three years following adoption of the Act, the federal share "shall not exceed 90 per centum of the costs . . . and thereafter shall not exceed 50 per centum of such costs. . . ." While it is hard to believe that the federal share will shrink to 50 percent so quickly, that is the language of the Act.

This suggests that any church or religious agency seeking to develop an anti-poverty program with federal aid should be prepared to pay one half of the costs after mid-1967. Thus far there is little evidence that the churches have taken this into consideration in their budget-planning.

If this change in the percentage of the federal contribution does occur, what will be the response of the churches? Can they say, "This program merited a high priority in our own planning when we had to pay only ten percent of the cost (and often could do this without any direct cash outlay), but it does not merit our continued participation if we have to pay one half of the cost"? Do the churches have different stewardship standards for the expenditures of church dollars than they have for the allocation of federal dollars?

Several churchmen respond to this change in the federal share by saying, "The churches and the denominational agencies simply will have to allocate a bigger slice of their financial resources to the anti-poverty programs that have been undertaken by the churches." This simple declaratory statement overlooks two other factors. First of all, at the same point in history when there will be demands for more churches dollars for the war on poverty, the denominations and local churches will be confronted with requests for larger appropriations for higher education and for new church development. The burgeoning enrollments in church-related colleges and universities will be the basis for one demand. The rapid increase in the number of new families being formed and the new housing boom will be used to document the need for more money for church extension.

While some churchmen may expect that the war on poverty

will receive first priority in the allocation of denominational dollars, this is unlikely. The middle-class orientation of American Protestantism combined with the normal pressures for institutional survival and the accepted place of higher education and new church development mean that it will be extremely difficult to resist requests for appropriation increases for these two programs.

The difficulty of mobilizing large quantities of church dollars to replace federal grants in the churches' war on poverty also can be seen in the fact that denominational budgets for 1966 and 1967 included practically nothing for anti-poverty efforts. The churches' war on poverty has yet to be institutionalized in denominational budgeting procedures. Until it is institutionalized in the budget it will be very difficult to secure large appropriations for this effort.

The third aspect of the financial question may be the most controversial of all. There have been launched across America, under the community action program of OEO, several attempts to change the structure of society or at least to alter the distribution of power. Some of these are church-sponsored ventures and many of them have been subsidized by an OEO grant. Most of them come under the general classification of community organization and are directed toward giving the poor a larger share in the community decision-making process and accelerating the pace of social change. If successful, their very success probably will mean that it will be politically impossible for OEO to provide continued financial support. There will, however, be a need for continuing financial support from outside sources and, since the churches were the sponsors, the churches will be expected to provide larger financial grants. Where will the churches find this money? Will it be possible for conservative denominational agencies to finance organizations described and denounced by opponents as "revolutionary"? Will the sponsoring churches have to drop out of these programs and organizations because of lack of money? It is only a slight exaggeration to ask, who will finance the continuation of this revolution initiated by the churches and others with federal subsidies?

Where Should the Emphasis Be Placed?

One of the characteristics of the typical American Protestant church is to place great emphasis on a ministry to children and youth. Nearly every pulpit committee seeking a pastor places high on the list of qualifications the ability "to work with young people." Every adult churchman appears to want to be able to be proud of the youth program in his church. The older the member, the greater seems to be his concern that his church be able to "reach the young people."

This same unbiblical emphasis on tomorrow to the neglect of today's adult generation has been repeated in the federally financed war on poverty. According to OEO statistics the number of needy persons 65 and over is approximately equal to the number of needy youngsters in the 16-21 age bracket. During the first two years of operation OEO allocated $20,000,000 for special programs for the elderly compared to $800,000,000 for the Job Corps and the Neighborhood Youth Corps.

In August 1965, President Johnson announced a five-part

program employing 17,600 elderly citizens at a cost of $41,000,000. Seven months later only one of the five programs —the "foster grandparents"—was in operation, and that one employed 1,200 golden agers in 21 communities. The allocation for this program had been reduced from $10,000,000 to $5,500,000.

In the meantime the churches either were sitting out the war completely or devoting most of their energies to programs for children and youth.

While it is true that one of the major motivations for developing the federal anti-poverty program was to take some of the potential explosiveness out of the social dynamite in the slums, it is also true that the elderly are among the most seriously injured victims of poverty.

While it is true that many adults do voluntarily scrimp and sacrifice and spend their mature years in poverty in order to provide better opportunities for their children, it is also true that society frequently has benefited from this sacrificial effort. There is also the question raised by Mrs. Geneva Mathiasen, executive director of the National Council on the Aging, "as to whether voluntary self-denial should be elevated to the status of national policy."

While it is probably true that the economic return on an investment in a nineteen-year-old unemployed dropout will be greater than the economic return on an investment in a sixty-seven-year-old poverty-stricken adult, it is also true that all decisions in a Great Society cannot be made on purely economic considerations. There is also a real question as to how the churches can reconcile this pattern of economic decision-making with the biblical doctrine of man.

The churches must share the blame for this serious imbalance in the national anti-poverty effort.

Closely related is the emphasis that has been placed on employment and job training. Here again the churches have been strangely silent and have neglected an extremely serious question. From the very beginning the OEO and other federal and local agencies have placed a major emphasis on solving poverty through preparing people for jobs. As a result of pressure from Congress and the business community, this emphasis has been increased.

This emphasis on eliminating poverty by upward mobility through education and vocational training has continued in the face of the fact that one half of the poor live in households headed by a full-time worker whose wages are too low to support a family. For many of these people the answer to the problem of poverty is a higher minimum wage. While it is true that some of these employed heads of households could move up the economic ladder by upgrading their skills, this only means that someone else will be recruited to take that low-paying job in the hospital or the service trades and will be sentenced to a life of poverty. There is a difference between breaking the cycle of poverty for one family and eliminating the causes of poverty.

Another large group of the Americans living in poverty are people who are not eligible for the labor force and who cannot be brought into the labor market. This group includes the aged, the physically and mentally handicapped, the husbandless mothers of small children, and the children themselves. Full employment or vocational training will not move

138

these millions of Americans out of the blight and despair of poverty.

Here again is a serious question which has been largely neglected by the churches as they debate their role in the war on poverty.

To their credit the churches have been active in helping to correct the imbalance between rural and urban areas. Despite the fact that nearly one half of the people living in poverty reside in rural areas, the major emphasis of the governmental attack on poverty has been directed to urban centers. In part this imbalance is a result of the inadequacy of rural local governments and the inactivity of the state governments, in part it is a result of goals of the original federal program which was oriented to young people in urban slums, in part it is a product of the high visibility and concentration of poverty in cities, and in part it is due to the fact that urban poverty appears to be easier to treat than rural poverty.

Despite the significant efforts of the churches to deal with the problems of rural poverty, an imbalance still exists, and the emphasis of the national effort still is on urban poverty.

Raising this question about where the emphasis should be placed in the national anti-poverty effort immediately poses some basic policy questions for the churches. Should the churches allocate their limited resources to the areas being neglected by governmental agencies? Or should the churches direct their efforts to altering the emphasis of the national effort and correcting this imbalance which neglects the elderly, the unemployable, and the rural poor? Or should the churches concentrate their resources in those programs where the largest governmental subsidy is available?

What Are the Goals?

Perhaps the point of greatest neglect and the place where the churches could make their largest contribution is on the issue of goals. While the general goal of eliminating "the paradox of poverty in the midst of plenty in this Nation by opening to everyone the opportunity for education and training, the opportunity to work, and the opportunity to decency and dignity" was articulated in the declaration of purpose of the Economic Opportunity Act of 1964, very little energy has been directed toward the formulation of a systematic set of national goals for this war. This lack of specific goals has made it difficult to evaluate the effectiveness of the various anti-poverty programs. This lack of goals makes it impossible to develop a set of yardsticks for evaluation. [3]

The churches could make a major contribution to the war by working for a clearer statement of goals. This could begin by directing attention to the generalized goal stated in the Act itself. This is an inadequate statement. It begins by stating that the purpose of the Act is to eliminate the "paradox of poverty," but then goes on to suggest that this

[3] For an excellent analysis of this problem of goals, see S. M. Miller and Martin Rein, "The War on Poverty: Perspectives and Prospects," in Ben B. Seligman, ed., *Poverty as a Public Issue* (New York: The Free Press, 1965), pp. 272-320.

140

can be accomplished by education, training, and additional employment opportunities. As suggested earlier, such an approach is inadequate. Education, vocational training, and the creation of more jobs will enable millions of people to move up out of the ranks of poverty. Millions of others, however, who cannot enter the labor force will be left behind. A broader program is needed if poverty is to be eliminated. The actual goal of the current program is for the reduction, not the elimination, of poverty.

In its report the Ad Hoc Committee on the Triple Revolution stated an anti-poverty goal which is both more inclusive and more specific, "to provide every individual and every family with an adequate income as a matter of right." While this goal may not win widespread support, it does have the advantage of specificity. A goal such as this says very clearly that new economic approaches are needed and that simply enlarging educational and vocational opportunities will not produce the desired result.

A more adequate set of national goals is needed before it will be possible to have a constructive national debate on the appropriate methods and techniques for solving the problems of poverty. The churches can help create the climate that will produce more realistic goals.

A second approach to the question of goals that is open to the church is to concentrate attention on the *process* of goal formulation as well as on the content of the goals.

This process usually begins with a definition of *the problem*. While there still remains room for refinement, the problem has been adequately described by Harrington, Weller, Or-

141

shansky, Seligman, Kolko, Miller, and others.[4] This part of the process has been taking place for five years and is well advanced. The problem has been defined.

The second part of the process consists of an *analysis of the causes* of the problem and of the conditions that must be changed before the problem can be solved. Considerable public discussion also has occurred at this point in the process. Many critics argue that poverty is a product of a low level of national economic activity. Others contend that poverty is caused by lack of power. Some argue that the causes of poverty are inherited or can be traced to racial or cultural characteristics. A few insist that poverty is caused simply by an inadequate income. Many other explanations of the causes of poverty could be listed to illustrate the lack of a national consensus at this point in the process.

Without greater agreement on the causes of the problem it becomes impossible to move effectively into the third phase of the process which is the actual formulation of a general goal that is appropriate to the statement of the problem, and the articulation of specific goals that are consistent with the causes. Will the goal of enabling the powerless to acquire power solve the problem? Will a guaranteed

[4] Michael Harrington, *The Other America* (New York: The Macmillan Company, 1962); Jack E. Weller, *Yesterday's People* (Frankfort: University of Kentucky Press, 1965); Mollie Orshansky, "Counting the Poor: Another Look at the Poverty Profile," *Social Security Bulletin,* January, 1965; Ben B. Seligman, *Poverty as a Public Issue* (New York: The Free Press, 1965); Gabriel Kolko, *Wealth and Power in America* (New York: Frederick A. Praeger, 1962); Herman P. Miller, *Rich Man, Poor Man* (New York: Thomas Y. Crowell Company, 1964).

minimum annual income solve it? Will the goal of increased job opportunities produce a solution?

Until there is greater agreement on causes it will be difficult to formulate specific program goals that can win consensus support. Without wide public support for specific goals it is impossible to expect broad general agreement on the methods or techniques that should be employed to achieve these specific program goals.

The strong disagreement in the early years of this new war over tactics, strategies, and weapons is a result of this lack of a consensus on goals. It is unreasonable to expect a strong unified national anti-poverty effort until there is greater agreement on causes and goals.

As usual the churches have been very articulate in helping to define the problem and in focusing public attention on this phase of the goal formulation process. They have been much less helpful in the efforts to describe the causes of the problem or in the formulation of specific program goals.

The churches could supplement their contributions to the goal formulation process by devoting more attention to the development of a consistent Christian statement on poverty. Comparatively little effort has been devoted to this in the churches.[5] The decision-making process within the churches is still greatly influenced by the eighteenth- and nineteenth-century Protestant ethic which related poverty to sinfulness

[5] Two notable exceptions to this generalization are Henry Clark, *The Christian Case Against Poverty* (New York: Association Press, 1965), and Byron L. Johnson, *Need Is Our Neighbor* (New York: Friendship Press, 1966).

and prosperity to righteousness. Perhaps it is unreasonable to expect that the churches can focus public attention on these other neglected issues until after they have developed a consistent theological position on poverty. Even this will be insufficient unless Christians, both clergy and lay, believe in and act on these convictions. Perhaps the church must examine its own call before it can speak to the world on the neglected issues in the war on poverty.

8

The Call to the Churches

What is the Lord calling the churches to be and to do in this new war on poverty? To call attention to the neglected issues? To carry on their own war? To enter into an alliance with the federal government? The varying reactions of the churches suggest there is not a consensus on the answer to this question.

One response to this fundamental question would be to begin on the assumption that the churches may have a unique role in this war. This assumes that the churches are different from the other structures of society such as government, or the secular voluntary health and welfare agencies, or labor unions, or business organizations. This also assumes that the call to the churches is dictated by God rather than by the Office of Economic Opportunity or the local community action program. This assumes that the *primary* elements of the churches' call can be discovered by looking at the nature of the church rather than by examining the nature of the problem. This assumption will produce disturbing tensions and conflicts as the people in the churches seek to be guided in their actions by this definition of the nature of the church while those outside the churches will expect the response of the churches to be determined by the nature of the problem. The inevitable result is a tension-producing difference of opinion over goals, strategy, tactics, and weapons. This tension and these conflicts should not be feared. They are always present when the church is faithful to its Lord and its call.

While it is unreasonable to expect that any one statement on the call to the churches will win universal support among Christians, it may be helpful to use a five-part definition of the call in discussing the role of the churches in the war on poverty.

1. Be Present

The dominant New Testament image of the church is servanthood. To be an effective and useful servant, one has to be present. It is difficult to be a good servant *in absentia.* This suggests that the churches must be present with and among the poor. Such a suggestion is completely consistent with the teachings of the Old Testament prophets, with the ministry of Jesus, with the historical account of the New Testament church, and with the work and teachings of the reformers. The call is to be present—and to be present in a spirit of love.

A primary call to the church is to be present with the poor and to identify with them and their plight. The call is to be present with the low-paid dishwasher in the steaming kitchen of the fancy restaurant, with the harried mother of three tiny children as she waits her turn in the crowded waiting room at the public health clinic, with the relief clients as they wait in line in the hot sun to receive their food stamps, and with the unemployed father of six as he tramps the streets looking for work, for any kind of work.

The call to the church is to be present to fill the gaps in the anti-poverty program, to do those things and meet those needs which the government and the secular agencies cannot do or do not choose to do.

The call is to be present when governmental agencies are considering and evaluating their anti-poverty programs and to support new constructive and creative proposals, to suggest reforming or scraping old programs that have become irrelevant, and to press for the greatest possible degree of involvement of the poor in this process of governmental decision-making. The call is to be present as a watchdog, as a critic, as a supporter, and as enabler.

The call is to be present and to be a redemptive agent as efforts, both private and public, are made to enable the poor to realize their God-given potential. The call is to be there in a spirit of love as a supportive and redemptive force in the midst of the sea of hopelessness, despair, apathy, and pessimism which so often drowns those who seek to overcome the blight of poverty. In being present the churches can help the poor regain the dignity which has been taken from them.

2. Be Faithful

All around one can find the cries of soldiers in the war on poverty, "Victory over poverty!" "Power for the powerless!" "Wipe out the causes of poverty!"

This excitement can divert the churches from their primary

call. The call to the churches is not to be large or to be successful or to be powerful or to be dispensers of material wealth. The call to the churches is to be faithful and obedient. The call is to reenact the crucifixion.

When debating their role in the war the churches must be guided by this call to be faithful to the gospel and to respond in terms of the unique gift the churches have to offer. When selecting the weapons to be used in this war, the churches must be guided, not by the choice of weapons made by the "enemy," but rather by selecting those courses of action that are consistent with a gospel of love. In actions as well as in admonitions the churches must be faithful to the message they proclaim.

This call to faithfulness also will produce tensions. When the Christian social-concerns committee of the conference, synod, or diocese comes out publicly in favor of a higher minimum wage, the trustees of the local church-related hospital may oppose such a move because of the effect on the hospital budget. When a group of churchmen urge that a new ministry be undertaken in a poverty-stricken neighborhood, there will be objections from those who contend, "We have a policy that we will not start a new congregation anywhere unless we can expect it to be financially self-supporting within four years." When a church group moves in to build housing for low-income families, there will be opposition from those who argue, "The church should be the church and leave housing to private enterprise and the government." When the poor who have been aided by the church in their struggle to gain a voice in the community decision-making process turn on the leaders of the church and attack them for their failures, some churchmen will cry, "See how ungrateful they are! Let's get out of this anti-poverty business and go back to the real business of the church."

3. Be Competent

As the churches seek to be faithful servants among the poor, many become involved in providing services to the poor. These services range from job training programs in the Neighborhood Youth Corps to legal clinics, from classes for preschoolers to family-planning clinics, from literacy programs for adults to housing for low-income families. As they participate in each of these activities the churches are under a mandate to be competent. They should hold themselves to the same high standards of performance that is expected of governmental and other secular agencies in this war.

Unfortunately this has not always happened. Several of the church-sponsored ventures in housing have been poorly conceived and poorly managed. Some of the OEO-financed anti-poverty programs administered by the churches have been extremely high-cost ventures marked by inadequate planning and poor administration. The fact that these same criticisms can be leveled at parallel efforts by secular agencies is not an acceptable excuse.

This same call for excellence extends to all the efforts of the churches. When the churches venture into the political arena to influence the decision-making processes, they should be equipped with skill and expertise. A cloak of righteousness is not sufficient. The call is not to be successful, but that does not mean that failure because of incompetence is automatically excused. Too often this call for competence is misunderstood as an argument that the churches should stay out of the political arena. This is not accurate. To be faithful to the gospel the churches must be involved in all facets of human life and society including the places where political and governmental decisions are made. In responding, the churches should bring both their presence and a degree of competence into the decision-making process.

This call to be competent also extends into the area of social justice. It means that the churches should understand the issues and, especially, be able to anticipate the consequences of a given course of action. This failure to accurately anticipate the consequences often is the greatest single weakness in the churches' response to a social, economic, or political issue.

This call to be competent also means that the churches should be creative in developing new ideas and methods of achieving the goal. For example, the formation of church-sponsored housing cooperatives may not only be a useful means of helping to solve the housing problem, it may also be one of the most creative means of achieving greater participation by the poor.

4. Be Honest

Closely related to the need to be faithful is the call to be honest. In this war the churches must not promise more than they can deliver, they must keep faith with their allies and they must avoid deceit and deception.

The churches are confronted with the problem of credibility. Too many people do not believe what the churches have to say. For both theological and pragmatic reasons the churches must be honest both in their relationships with the poor and in their relationships with the enemies of the poor.

This is a difficult call to heed. When the enemy does not hesitate to lie, cheat, deceive, vilify, and steal, there is a tremendous temptation to resort to the same weapons—"to fight fire with fire." When the churches fall prey to this temptation, they are no longer faithful to their call. They also lose much of their power and influence with their friends and allies.

5. *Be Prophetic*

One of the clearest calls to the churches in this new war is to speak with a prophetic voice. The churches are being called to lift up poverty as a moral issue.

Perhaps the first phase of this task is to point out that the social and economic problems of the day are also great moral issues. There is a moral imperative to this war on poverty. The churches have been very effective in recent years in calling attention to the moral issue in racial discrimination. Now there is a need to do the same with the problem of poverty. Only a beginning has been made in response to this call.

The war on poverty, however, is not the only place at which the prophetic voice of the churches should be heard. The churches should be helping to set the moral tone of our society. Poverty and racial discrimination are but two of the problems that require solutions that can come only from within a context of moral values. The problem of hunger is a moral problem, but so is the problem of lack of dignity and self-esteem.

The churches also are called to a prophetic role as they seek to be objective critics of the war on poverty and of the various anti-poverty programs. One of the central arguments against the churches seeking OEO grants is that this may inhibit their prophetic participation.

When the churches are secure in their call, it will be comparatively easy for them to decide on the appropriate type and degree of involvement in the war on poverty. There is every reason to believe that this response will continue to be varied. Some churches will conclude in terms of their call that they must enlist immediately while others will decide that their call prohibits direct participation. Some will direct their response to one element of the call while others will undertake a multi-faceted approach to the war. Some will identify firmly with the powerless and freely engage in conflict with those whom the poor identify as the enemy. Others will stand as a reconciling force between conflicting and competing elements of society, between the governed and those who govern, between the haves and the have-nots. Some churches will seek to reform the structures of society while others will try to replace them with a new and more egalitarian system.

As long as the response of the churches is determined *primarily* by the definition of the nature of the churches and *secondarily* by the nature of the problem, there is good reason to expect that the churches will carry their share of the load in this new war on poverty.

Suggestions for Further Reading

Bagdikian, Ben H. *In the Midst of Plenty*. New York: New American Library, 1964.

Bluestein, Iris W. "Housing-Poverty War Relationships," *Journal of Housing* (June, 1966).

Carothers, J. Edward. *Keepers of the Poor*. New York: Board of Missions of The Methodist Church, 1966.

Clark, Henry. *The Christian Case Against Poverty*. New York: Association Press, 1965.

Cloward, Richard A. and Piven, Frances Fox. "A Strategy To End Poverty," *The Nation* (May 2, 1966).

The Concept of Poverty. Washington: Chamber of Commerce of the United States, 1965.

Everett, Robinson O., ed. "Antipoverty Programs," *Law and Contemporary Problems*. Durham, N. C.: Duke University School of Law (Winter, 1966).

Fishman, Leo, ed. *Poverty Amid Affluence*. New Haven: Yale University Press, 1966.

153

Gans, Herbert J. *The Urban Villagers*. New York: The Free Press, 1962.

Graybeal, David M. *Can't We All Be Rich?* New York: Friendship Press, 1966.

Jacobs, Paul and Landau, Saul. *The New Radicals*. New York: Random House, 1966.

Johnson, Byron L. *Need Is Our Neighbor*. New York: Friendship Press, 1966.

Keyserling, Leon H. *Progress or Poverty*. Washington: Conference on Economic Progress, 1964.

Kolko, Gabriel. *Wealth and Power in America*. New York: Frederick A. Praeger, 1962.

May, Edgar. *The Wasted Americans*. New York: Harper & Row, 1964.

Miller, Richard P. *Rich Man, Poor Man*. New York: New American Library, 1964.

Morgan, James N. *Income and Welfare in the United States*. New York: McGraw Hill Book Company, 1962.

Office of Policy Planning and Research, United States Department of Labor. *The Negro Family*. Washington: The Government Printing Office, 1965. This is the widely discussed and extremely controversial "Moynihan Report."

Ornati, Oscar. *Poverty amid Affluence*. New York: The Twentieth Century Fund, 1966.

Pearl, Arthur and Riessman. *New Careers for the Poor*. New York: The Free Press, 1965.

Peltigrew, Thomas F. *A Profile of the Negro American*. Princeton: D. Van Nostrand Company, 1964.

Poverty and Deprivation in the United States. Washington: Conference on Economic Progress, 1962.

Schaller, Lyle E. "Church Sponsorship of Housing," *Journal of Housing* (April, 1966).

———. *Community Organization: Conflict and Reconciliation*. Nashville: Abingdon Press, 1966.

Seligman, Ben B., ed. *Poverty as a Public Issue*. New York: The Free Press, 1965.

Silberman, Charles E. *Crisis in Black and White*. New York: Random House, 1964.

Simon, Arthur. *Faces of Poverty*. St. Louis: Concordia Publishing House, 1966.

Theobald, Robert. *The Challenge of Abundance*. New York: New American Library, 1961.

Weisbrod, Burton A., ed. *The Economics of Poverty*. Englewood Cliffs, N. J.: Prentice-Hall, 1965.

Weller, Jack E. *Yesterday's People*. Frankfort: University of Kentucky Press, 1965.

INDEX

157